THE JIM LEHRER

LEHRER

PLAYS

Published by Plays Inverse Press
Pittsburgh, PA
www.playsinverse.com

ISBN 13: 978-0-9997247-2-9

First Printing: May 2018
Cover art by Friese Undine
Page and cover design by Tyler Crumrine
Printed in the U.S.A.

PLAYS
INVERSE

THE JIM LEHRER PLAYS

MICKLE MAHER

PLAYS INVERSE PRESS
PITTSBURGH, PA
2018

To Diana and Colm.

THE JIM LEHRER PLAYS

THE
STRANGERER

"I was in Crawford and I said I was looking for a book to read and Laura said you oughta try Camus. I also read three Shakespeares."
— *George W. Bush*

The Strangerer was first produced in 2007 by Theater Oobleck at the Chopin Theater in Chicago, with the following cast:

President Bush   Guy Massey
Senator Kerry   Mickle Maher
Jim Lehrer   Colm O'Reilly

CHARACTERS:
President George W. Bush
Senator John Kerry
Jim Lehrer, news anchor

(The set is much the same as the set of the presidential debate of 2004 at the University of Miami's Convocation Center: two lecterns, a moderator's desk, all with microphones, and a bright red carpet. The carpet, however, is a square and it defines the playing space absolutely. Beyond its edges is darkness. No one leaves the carpet until the end.)

(Lehrer is at his desk when the audience comes in, shuffling his papers, adjusting his suit, etc., in preparation for broadcast.)

LEHRER
Ninety seconds to air. *(To audience:)* Everybody okay?

(Thirty second pause.)

One minute. *(To audience:)* Thank you all very much—in advance. We're going to have a great debate.

(Thirty second pause.)

Thirty seconds. We are now gone to our "mute mode."

(Thirty second pause.)

Good evening from the University of Miami Convocation Center in Coral Gables, Florida. I'm Jim Lehrer of "The NewsHour" on PBS.

And I welcome you to the first of the 2004 presidential debates between President George W. Bush, the Republican nominee, and Senator John Kerry, the Democratic nominee.

These debates are sponsored by the Commission on

Presidential Debates.

Tonight's will last ninety minutes, following detailed rules of engagement worked out by representatives of the candidates. I have agreed to enforce their rules on them.

The umbrella topic is foreign policy and homeland security, but the specific subjects were chosen by me, the questions were composed by me, the candidates have not been told what they are, nor has anyone else.

For each question there can only be a two-minute response, a ninety-second rebuttal and, at my discretion, a discussion extension of one minute.

Candidates may not direct a question to each other. There will be two-minute closing statements but no opening statements.

There is an audience here in the hall, but they will remain absolutely silent for the next ninety minutes, except for now, when they join me in welcoming President Bush and Senator Kerry.

> (The sound of applause. Bush and Kerry come on stage, shake hands, take their places at the lecterns.)

LEHRER
Good evening, Mr. President; Senator Kerry.

As determined by a coin toss, the first question goes to you, Senator Kerry. You have two minutes.

Do you believe you could do a better job than President Bush in preventing another 9/11-type terrorist attack on the United States?

KERRY
Yes, I do.

But before I answer further, let me thank you for moderating. I want to thank the University of Miami for hosting us. And I know the president will join me in welcoming all of Florida to this debate. You've been through the roughest weeks anybody could imagine. Our hearts go out to you. And we admire your pluck and perseverance. I can make America safer than President Bush has made us.

(Bush takes out a knife and approaches Lehrer's desk. He stabs Lehrer in the back. Lehrer collapses. Bush steps back. Lights fade slowly to black, as a softly dramatic, melancholic closing theme plays over the sound of a rising wind. After a brief blackout: lights up. Lehrer is back at his table, the candidates at their lecterns.)

LEHRER
Good evening, again. Again, I'm Jim Lehrer of "The NewsHour" on PBS and this is the first of the 2004 presidential debates sponsored by the Commission on Presidential Debates between President George W. Bush, and Senator John Kerry.

If you're just joining us, or if you've been with us to this point, some explanation is in order. We've just returned from a blackout—if that is the correct term—a blackout of the lights, accompanied by music and the sound of wind, here on the Convocation Center's stage. A blackout which was immediately preceded by President Bush leaving his lectern, approaching me with a knife, and stabbing me with that knife between my shoulder blades, appearing to draw the blade down my spine to the small of my back.

Now, above all it should be made clear: the knife that you saw, the knife President Bush appeared to murder me with, was not an actual knife. It was a prop. A stage knife, in fact, if that is the term used by, uh, stage people. Without my prior knowledge, it was agreed upon by the candidates and their representatives that this debate should open with a staged murder followed by a blackout. It was also agreed upon by the candidates and their representatives that I was to be the "murder victim." But I should stress: in no way was I actually harmed. I did not die, nor did I approach death. At no time did I lose consciousness. When the president initially advanced upon me with the knife, I felt some small surprise. But I'm something of an expert on knives—I have an extensive collection of knives in my home—and I realized almost immediately that the knife in the president's hand was not real. And so I played along. I "play-acted," if that is the term. I was brutally "murdered" by President Bush and the lights went to black.

I should also emphasize that the mystery of the president's action does not bear in any way on this evening's proceedings. The topic this evening is foreign policy, not the question of why the president would stage a theatrical attack on a seasoned, even-handed member of the press on national television before a live audience. It is a mystery which for the purposes of this debate must be content to remain a mystery.

The question, again, was to you, Senator Kerry. Two minutes. Do you believe you could do a better job than President Bush in preventing another 9/11-type terrorist attack on the United States?

KERRY
Yes, Jim, I can make America safer than President Bush has made us. And I believe President Bush and I both love

our country equally. But we just have a different set of convictions about how you make America safe.

(Bush pulls out a handgun, strides over to Lehrer, takes aim and fires, once. Lehrer clutches his chest, gasps, falls onto the floor. Bush then fires four shots into his prostrate body. The "blackout music" and wind begin, as before, and the lights slowly begin to fade. Blackout. After a moment: lights up. Lehrer back at his desk, the candidates at their lecterns.)

LEHRER
And again, good evening. I'm Jim Lehrer and this is the first of the 2004 presidential debates between President George W. Bush and Senator John Kerry. And if you're just joining us, or you've been with us to this point, an explanation: We've just returned for the second time from a blackout. A blackout, accompanied by music and the sound of wind. Time has passed. In that time I have refreshed myself with some crackers and juice. I was in need of refreshment because when we were last visible, President Bush left his lectern, stood approximately three yards from my desk and drew from his suit jacket what appeared to be an actual handgun. He aimed it at me, fired one time and, after I collapsed, fired four more times at my motionless, prostrate body. Well. It was not an actual gun. It was a starter's pistol. With blanks, not bullets. As with the "murder" of myself which began this debate, this, as well, was a staged murder. However, unlike that first murder of myself, on this occasion at no point prior to the firing of the false gun did I come to an awareness that it was, indeed, false. I have no in-depth knowledge of guns or ammunition, only knives. My floor-to-ceiling collection of knives fills my entire apartment, so there's no possibility, indeed there is no space to be made for the collection of firearms or anything else.

So despite my recent experience with an all-in-good-fun stage death, when President Bush leveled the barrel at me I believed what anyone ignorant of the difference between a true gun and a trick gun would believe. I believed, quite reasonably, that the president was going to shoot me through the face at close range and I went into something of a panic. I had a slight seizure, which you witnessed, but I'm all right now. And ready to go on—if we're all of us ready. Yes? All right. Again, let's continue with Senator Kerry's response to my first question, for which I'll grant him the full two minutes. Senator Kerry, once more: do you believe you—

(During the above, Bush has gotten hold of a pillow and is slowly advancing on Lehrer.)

LEHRER
Excuse me—Mr. President, I would ask that you—look, no more. No more of this.

(Lights begin to fade. Music; wind.)

No! No! Leave the lights!

(Bush has the pillow over Lehrer's face. Pushes him down onto the desk. Lehrer struggles, gets hold of the pillow, pulls away. There is a tug of war with the pillow. Music continues, lights dimming still.)

Leave the lights! Leave the lights!

BUSH
AHHHHHHGGHHH!

(Lights up, quickly. Bush gives up on the pillow, sulks back to his lectern. Lehrer returns to his desk as music

comes to an end.)

LEHRER
All right... let's just go on to the next question. How about that? Yes? Move forward. All right? All right. Mr. President, to you. Two minutes. Does the Iraq experience make it more likely or less likely that you would take the United States into another preemptive military action?

BUSH
(Pause.) Mr. Lehrer, were you aware that I am a lover of the theater? No, you were not aware. It is for the reason that I do love it that it is kept a secret. Maybe you noticed it is an unspoken government policy to keep secret whatever an elected official might truly love. Feel passion of. Even in the case of our family or country or dog we are advised to speak of our love for these things in only the most transparently artificial and hollow fashion. Don't know where I would be at without my love of the theater. Would be a person outside of love.

But the point is here: as a theater lover I last night went out to seeing a play at one of Coral Gables' very old and grandish theaters. And at a specific moment in that play, a thought—it didn't occur to me, it came, it flowered up into me. As a result of this specific theatrical moment, it bloomered into me the thought that it didn't matter if I, uh, murdered in some fashion the modulator of this debate. Was not important if I committed the homicide of you. There out of the heat, out of the footlights and the people all packed in there in the seats and aisles was this thought sprung. Baked up.

And I walked all night with this thought, walked the city with this thought. Ended up on the beach. And as the sun came up with its mosquitoes coming out of it this thought sort of was drifted aside by a question. And that question was "what is the manner to be?" The manner of your demising. Because if it's no importance that we do away with you, the only thing that could of any possibility appear to be important is the style and method—the manner in which you are done away. Because that's what makes us people. The manner in which we go about killing other people.

There's such a multivariable ways.

And so I have rehearsed with the, uh, knife, the gun. Pillow. And, yes, they did not, uh, did not receive the desired, uh—acceptable response from out there. I understand that. But it's hard work, rehearsal. Hard work. And be awares my opponent was of no help. Stood there. Backstage had no—offered no ideas. Because my opponent, this is not a priority of him. Last night at the play, said it was. Now says this is the wrong place, wrong time. But I think as a leader you have to make a choice. NOW. On the manner. I mean, people should like it. I understand that. The murder moment of you should be enjoyable.

Like last night, this play, its moment, there was a standing, uh... stand up applause. Hats in the air. And that's what I intempt to accomplish. But how to accomplish? I have rehearsed by doing—knife, gun, pillow... I will now rehearse by talking. And I think if only I can now talk the story of that moment, how it came into me there, then I'll know of the action to be taken here. So I will tell that story. As best as I are able. I will talk in my turn and you will all listen. And if I talk rather good and you all listen good, listen strong and resolute, then we will understand how a theater moment was made and can then be makers of our own. Our own moment. The killing of Jim Lehrer. Tonight, on this stage.

LEHRER
Senator Kerry, ninety second response.

KERRY
Jim, the president is just flat wrong when he says that the killing of you is not a priority for me. It is my number one priority. And I also agree with the president—I agreed with him last night after the play and all of today—that the manner in which we kill you is the issue. Indeed, what else tonight besides the manner of Jim Lehrer's execution could be of interest to any man? I have been consistent in that position. Where I and the president differ is on the matter of when and where. He claims that his experience of a moment in the play we saw last night compels him to want to kill you on this stage, tonight.

Well, I was with the president last night—picked him up, drove him through the ruins of the city, and sat with him through the play. But the moment in that play which, the president claims, created such an urgency in him to murder you on this night and on this stage, that moment, for me, just didn't work. The reason being simply that during that moment I was asleep. And as those among our audience who have experienced sleep or even near sleep know, in a state of sleep or even near sleep, especially in the theater, the events of the waking world have significantly less definition and impact. Do you sleep, Jim?

LEHRER
No, I do not.

KERRY
I didn't think so. I, myself, do sleep and have slept many times. I sleep as often as possible. I was asleep standing outside the president's hotel room, car keys in my hand, listening to him fight with his mother. I slept while driving

us to the theater, I slept through most of the play and I am, in fact, asleep now. Annnd... thass *(Lets out a sigh and mumblings of a sleep talker, and then:)* But my point is this: if this theatrical moment the president speaks of had half the punch he claims it had, how could I have slept through it? How compelling could it have been? We were in the front row. Life doesn't work like that. To the important things, at least, we are connected. We are conscious. Look, the bottom line is my desire to commit senseless and arbitrary acts of violence is as strong as any man's, but we don't have to rush it. The knife, the gun, this pillow—they didn't work. We all felt it. Nothing genuine or memorable there at all. Jim, your execution, or, more precisely, the manner of your execution is a top priority for me. That's my promise to America. But we need to get the job done right.

BUSH
Can I respond to that?

LEHRER
Let's do one of these one-minute extensions. You have thirty seconds.

BUSH
Thank you, sir. Look, it's simple: we're at war. This is war. A war between Now and Later. My opponent takes the side of Later. I take Now. Because Now is real. It's, uh, it's happening right now. Later's a, a disabstraction. Last night, the moment I saw, that I experienced on that stage, they didn't do it Later. It worked because they did it right then. Which back then was Now. Sure the senator slept through it, but he was out in the lobby after, couldn't stop talking about how much he loved it. Changed his life, he said. Loved it. Now he says "wrong place, wrong time." Well, that's the wrong message.

LEHRER
Thirty seconds, Senator.

KERRY
Howw… izz that what yur wearing?… maubb… buh…

LEHRER
All right, next question to you, Senator Kerry. Two minutes. You just—you've repeatedly accused President Bush—not here tonight, but elsewhere before—of not telling the truth about Iraq, essentially of lying to the American people about Iraq. Give us some examples of what you consider to be his not telling the truth.

KERRY
Well, I've never, ever used the harshest word, as you did just then. And I try not to. But I'll nevertheless tell you that I think he has not been candid with the American people. And I'll tell you exactly how. The president just said that before this debate I offered no help in creating the staging for your murder. That's not true. I allowed him to practice on me, first with the knife, then the gun. The pillow, he didn't—that was a last-second impulse on his part. But the knife, the gun, we went over those together back in our green room, with him using me as a stand-in for you. Maybe he thinks I don't remember this because I was asleep. But I wasn't so asleep I couldn't feel a fake knife in my back, or hear the sound of that pistol. I'm asleep, not turned to clay. So it's not true that I've been no help tonight. But I'll tell you this: It was clear back there that none of his ideas were going to be dramatically effective. Knife, gun, pillow—it's hackneyed, we've all seen it before. But most importantly, even if any of his ideas had been stageworthy, the fact is that this is not a true theatrical stage. This is a stage for debates and symposia, for panel discussions, lectures and convocations. Dim lights and

spooky music and unwarranted homicide have no place here.

LEHRER
President Bush, ninety seconds.

BUSH
No place? Where else does he think—I mean, here are the hot lights. Sound system. Folks watching. This is the stage. And most important here there's, uh, uh, right here's Mr. Lehrer. Jim Lehrer. Can't do it without him. Makes no sen—I mean you can have the most dramatical stage in town and you don't have Jim Lehrer on it to—to decapulate or saw in half or what have you—makes no sense. He makes it the stage. This is the stage. And I am aware that, uh, the things I tried, uh, we have not succeeded as fast as we wanted to succeed. But we will. I will. Because I'm committed to—I love the theater. I love the theater. With those, uh… people, uh, characters, who talk, who talk in so articulate a way, who really express what they articulate so well, and then, uh, those same character-people, uh… maybe go around somewhere and do something and then, uh, then it's all over and they go off the stage. They go, and you can go, too, just like them, you just get up and leave. You're just like them. They go out one way, you go out the other. You're like them. I love that.

But make no doubt, it's hard work to get to a great moment on the stage. A moment that means something. Hard work all—from everybody involved. It's hard work for all of you just to get out, get away, to the theater. Then hard work to sit down, pay attention, and feel the appropriate feelings, and experience the theatrical moment in, in the same moment as it happens in the manner it occurs. But if I can—as I'm about to—tell the story of how I experienced that moment last night, and tell it correctly, then we will

all together understand the way forward in making this
moment tonight.

LEHRER
New question. Mr. President, two minutes. You have said
there was a, quote, "miscalculation" of what the conditions
would be in post-war Iraq. What was the miscalculation
and how did it happen?

BUSH
Okay, it all begins in my hotel room, last evening. Begins
with how I was having, uh, difficulty in getting out of that
hotel room. With my mom dead there. Did you—were
you aware of that? Yeah. Mom died today. Or yesterday,
maybe. Or maybe a few years ago, I don't know. Anyhow
she's dead now and never wants me going out leaving her
alone. Wants me to keep watch over her. The casket open,
how she likes it. I'd prefer it closed, screw it down. But
she says open and me there up all night, no coffee, sit up
straight. There's pressure. And last night, in the hotel, she's
in there, laid out, and she's made it clear: there's no choice.
I am to stay and keep watch. I think maybe I can put the
lid down, sneak out. I'd heard about a play, something of
quality, recommended. In Coral Gables. Wanted to see it.
So I think—just push down the lid. Get out. But she's
got her fingers on the, uh, the lip. Coffin edge. So I can't
close it. I try to shut it down, I try, but she's got her fingers
tight there like claws and eyes peeking out through her
knuckles, through the crack. So I flip it back up and I'm
stuck there. It's cold—she's got the air conditioner. Up.
Freezing. No coffee. I'm pulling my suit sleeves over my
hands. Sit up. Keep watch. Laura's out. Book club. But I'm
in with the, uh, dead mother's body, that's been my life.
Last few nights or few years, whatever it's been, that's been
my life. Dead body says don't go out. Dead body says "you
will not attend the theater." I love the theater. My secret

love. I love, uh... but she says "don't go." And it's getting
late. And, uh, to be honest I was starting to, uh—nervous,
shake. The evening was upon me. Darkness. The time of
theater, the time of... darkness descends, curtains rise up,
across the stages of the city, all over Coral Gables, this
great theatrical city, a city of great stagecraft, now in ruins.
Somewhere a curtain was, uh, was rising up on this play I
wanted to see. And I was not there. I was in the hotel with
my dead mom. Senator here was supposed to come and
pick me up any minute. But if I could not convince her,
there's trouble. So I said, said to her, "Now you're going to
let me go out tonight. I have stayed in over you, watched
over you, but tomorrow is the—I'm debating my opponent
and so must not show up smelling and looking like I've
been years now in close promiscuity with a cadaver. I must
appear a man who lives and enjoys his life." But my life—
there's a kind of a boundary between me and my life these
days, a wall which is not *death* but more in the person of
a *living corpse*. It is not death which divides me from my
life at this time it is a *living corpse* in the person of my *dead
mother*. That's unacceptable. And I said, "You're going to
let me go out and see a play." Well, she rises up out of her
silken quilting, raises up in her finery, best dress, pearls
rattling, sits up there in the, that casket I've been dragging
around the campaign trail, sits up and says no, no you will
not go. Not go into your life, out to your play in the ruin
of Coral Gables. There's no life out there, she says. Just a
carnaged city, just rubble and flames and sick water. Rats
and virasuls. You will not go, words burping up out of her
black corpse mouth. *You will not go.*

And maybe then I would not have gone, if my nerve had
failed, would not have gone and seen the play I saw with its
moment I saw and come to know that great moments on
the stage are pertainable. Would not have come to know
that. But my nerve did not fail. I took the candle up from

the foot of her casket there, held it up against her face, uh, and just said it very plainly: "I'm going out. Senator's picking me up." Her skin in the candlelight very smooth, embalmed. Gone brown around the lips. And out of that mouth she screams. Big scream. Big President's Dead Mother scream. And it goes on and on. And I realize there, standing there inside that scream that I, uh, there is just something fundamental about this world and the rules of this world that I don't understand. Don't understand why I'm expected to feel, uh, some... thing for a dead person. They're dead—she's dead. There could be a, a thousand dead people stacked up in that hotel room. I'd still... my choice would be to go out. See a play. I'm not embarrassed of that. And, uh, I wanted to, uh, explain this to her—but there's too much scream. Ing. You see how hard work this is? And I can hear, just behind me outside the door the senator shaking his car keys. Afraid to knock I guess. Enough talk—it's time to go. So inside that scream, that scream, uh, coming down on me, I back towards the door. Slow. And slip out. And that scream is still going—I can still hear it, even here. Heard it all night. But I was out. Freedom. I was out. And so began my evening.

LEHRER
Senator, ninety seconds.

KERRY
Jim, the president says that the reason I didn't knock on his hotel door while his dead mother was screaming at him is that I was afraid to knock. I wasn't afraid to knock. I was asleep. And the first rule of sleep is that if you find yourself standing before a closed door, and behind that door you hear a shrieking corpse, shrieking without cease, you do not open that door. Everyone knows this.

But more importantly, the president is trying to argue that

he needs to tell the story of our journey to the theater last night. He claims he needs to tell this story because it will clarify what that moment in the theater he experienced was and how it worked. That his dead mother and his experience with his dead mother, her scream, my shaking of my keys, our drive through the city and all that happened there, every detail of the evening in other words, he says, is of a piece with his experience of this "theater moment." That the chain of events that preceded his moment in the theater and his decision to eliminate you, Jim, have some coherence. That they're connected. But they're not connected. That I arrived at the same decision while being asleep the entire night is proof of that.

Who knows why we decide to kill other people? Whether awake or asleep such a choice swims into the heat and muddle of our thoughts with no sign of whence it came. I stood in that dim hallway, the scream coming through the door muffled by the thickness and warmth of the air around me, the carpet below me, and down the hall a dozen other doors, all closed, all with their own stories behind them, their own unhappy, screaming, clutching corpses who we will never know anything of. I might have knocked on any of these doors, and gone with someone else to another theater, or a restaurant, or a ramble through the hot wind and craters, and still come to this same conviction regarding your extermination. It's simply a conviction that came from nowhere, from the heat of the sky, the cool of the moon, who knows? All that matters is that I do have the conviction.

LEHRER
New question. Two minutes, Senator Kerry. What is your position on the whole concept of preemptive war?

KERRY

The president has the right, and always has had the right, for preemptive strike. But if and when you do it, Jim, you have to do it in a way that passes the test, that passes the global test where your countrymen, your people understand fully why you're doing what you're doing and you can prove to the world that you did it for legitimate reasons. It's all in how you conduct yourself. When we kill you, for example, if we go about it in the right way, if we're patient and deliberate, then America and the world will be with us. I believe that this evening is the wrong time and this stage is the wrong place; rather we need to step back and explore all the avenues before committing ourselves to a random, meaningless butchery. If we do it immediately, as the president seems to want to, in an entirely rash, go-it-alone, knife-gun-pillow manner, then nobody will be happy, least of all our audience. I contend they would be mystified, and like all mystified audiences, they would be bored, and being bored they would fall asleep. Then they would be asleep, I would be asleep, and you'd be dead, leaving the president as the only one on this stage and in this debate alive and conscious. And that's not what we want for this country.

LEHRER

Ninety seconds, Mr. President.

BUSH

All right, uh, I was outside the door, mom screaming. Senator's there in the hall, asleep, ready to go. Shaking his keys. So we, uh, there was the hallway, then the—we took the stairs. In the lobby I got him a soda to, uh, give—make him a little more pep, energy. *Didn't want him to sleep through the show.* Got my, uh, change from the machine. Went out to the car, rental car. Good car. Uh... good it was a rental because there's just that one big key, you know, not a lot of keys to fumble with, around. He's still asleep, don't want to have him fumble.

Which makes me wonder if he just had the one key, what was making the sound of keys shaking? He must have been just shaking that one key real hard.

See, being with the senator can be, uh, it's a strange experience. Because of his, uh, somnam—uh, his, uh— he's a zombie. So, uh, going out with him is strange because you're, uh, with him, but, uh, he's sleeping. So you're alone. You go out together with the senator, you're alone. Which is sometimes how I feel by myself. When I'm alone with myself. I'm alone. But right there is myself. So I'm not, uh, entirely the only one.

Are you with me, Mr. Lehrer?

LEHRER
Excuse me, sir?

BUSH
Are you with, uh—are you listening? Because he's out.

LEHRER
I believe I'm doing my best to listen, yes.

BUSH
But then, then you're paid to—you're a paid man to listen. You're paid to be here. What about all those other, uh, people, out there? Half of them are listening just to make fun, make a game of how I talk—how I make expression. My mis-communicable, uh, wrong words. My, uh. *(Pause.)* Pauses. *(Pause.)* In odd places. They're makin' fun. Other half always agrees with what I say and so is not listening because they think they know what I am going to say

and have already previously agreed. With it. So again I'm alone. LISTEN TO ME. LISTEN TO ME. YOU ARE GOING TO DIE TONIGHT. And, uh, it seems to me that you should be a good listener because of that fact. Not because you're paid to listen. I need a good listener. This is not a game. Iz'serious business. Or maybe it's not. But we must agree to treat it as serious.

LEHRER
New question, Mr. President. Two minutes. Has the war in Iraq been worth the cost of American lives, 1,052 as of today?

BUSH
Yeah, uh... so the senator gets in the car, starts the car, and we pull out onto the avenue. It's a beautiful night. There's stars through the, uh, smoke, uh, the smoke from the burning heaps of, uh, heaps. And, uh, packs of dogs, uh, running, eating stuff. And though it's all very "devastated" and—I feel free. I'm free. And freedom is good. I'm free and it's good. Senator asleep at the wheel, driving through the starry wreck of Coral Gables, this great city, great theatrical town. Stars above, uh, smeary—big smear across the sky. Still that scream of my mom, but fainter now. And there's screaming, sure, of other people. Maybe they're sick, hurt, but maybe just, heh-heh, crazy. Man walks by bleeding at his, uh, his groin. And flies, uh, flying over puddles of—there's water standing around everywhere like soup with, uh, rats floating. And I wonder what is maybe inside those rats? Because they're, uh, puffing—they're puffed out. And I think, I don't need to know that, the secret of that, what's inside a, a puffed rat. I am content with that being a secret. I'm free, driving. Going to a show. Play. The play's what's secret. The play's what's—the city's just ruins. No secrecy in that. The play's what's secret. What's it going to be? Am I going to like it? I'm excited by

that secret. Nothing on the radio. Just static in the night and stars and, uh, screams and, and uh, puffy, uh... this great city. Fantastic city. Everyone should be proud.

But to get back to the, uh, what I was saying. We came to a bridge. And we, the senator stops. And he looks at me says, uh, "I don't know where the theater is. I may have once known," he says, "but, uh, perhaps that was a dream, that knowledge." See, because he's in Dreamland? My opponent. Dreamland. Not reality. He doesn't know where it is, what direction.

But standing on the bridge, there in the night, is a young, uh, a little girl. There's a little girl there dressed all, all in black. African-American girl. Maybe six, maybe five years. Pearls around her throat, like my mom. Braids. Smoking a cigarette, smoking, very slowly. Leaning on the railing over the slow flow of water with the rats bumping up against the dead fish and bodies and she's, uh, she's singing. Very sultry, cabaret sort of song. Sad song. Maybe something about life, maybe something about death—that's what's so sad is you can't tell, can't tell which one it's about. It's a mystery, it's a secret. And I think, hey, she's got to know where the theater is. So I lean out the window and say, "Hey, do you know where the play is at?" But she keeps singing, even when the railing, uh,—it's corroded, maybe from the recent catastrophe, maybe from, uh, the, uh, railing inspectors dropping the ball, but it gives out and she's falling down in the canal. Startles up a little cloud of fleas, mosquitoes when she hits the water. Singing stops and, uh, and she cries a few times floating away, sinking. Then quiet again, everywhere. Just my mom's scream. Far away. My opponent and I watch the whole, uh, the singing, the falling, from inside the car. And I'm thinking, "Is maybe he jumping in after her? And is he thinking I'm going to? What's he thinking?" And "maybe she wanted to fall" is something else I think. Make her little splash of death inside all this bigger death. It was a moment that gave me a lot of thinking. Kind of filled up my head. See, the death of an innocent child will do that. It's terrible, a terrible thing, death of a—dead children. But it does give you—it opens up a big world of ideas. Where maybe there weren't ideas there before. So to answer your question, is it worth it? Well, every life is precious. But, uh, every death is precious, too. You think "that's terrible," but then you think, uh, other stuff. Didn't have that back at the hotel with my mom. Stuff, ideas. There's no idea in trying to push a coffin lid down on someone who wants it open. That's just a—there's no idea in that. That's the universal non-idea, coffin lid pushing down on a living corpse. There's no idea in your head when you're pushing down a coffin top on someone. Just "push." DOWN. Push. Push. Keep pushin'. KEEP PUSHIN'. DOWN.

LEHRER
Senator, ninety seconds.

KERRY
Jim, the president claims that I am in Dreamland. But while I won't run from the fact that I am asleep and being asleep I, like all Americans, occasionally dream, the idea that I am in Dreamland, that I am a resident of Dreamland, and my allegiance is therefore to Dreamland and not to the world of Reality is an outrageous claim. Who can say what is going on inside my head, inside any sleeper's head? Dreams, yes, certainly, at times, but Dreamland? Come on. When the president makes such a claim he is pretending a knowledge of secret things that neither he nor I—

BUSH
But this whole deal is about secret things.

LEHRER
Mr. President—

BUSH
Yeah. Secret how we're going to go about—kill this man.
Go about the business of death. Secret even to us. But I'd
like to, uh, you know—know.

(Bush steps out from behind his lectern, towards Lehrer.)

LEHRER
Mr. President—

BUSH
I NEED TO KNOW.

LEHRER
Please, President Bush...

BUSH
(Slowly advancing, holding his hands up to show that he has
no weapons.) It's all right, it's all right...

LEHRER
Mr. President, the debate—

BUSH
It's all right...

LEHRER
Why—please... please...

BUSH
(Suddenly jumps forward, assuming a martial arts stance.) SA!

(Lehrer yelps and jumps.)

Now see, was there something in—*what was it?* Element of—the surprising element? With my bare hands, with the Jew's jitsu, just jump up and tear your head off in a surprise? KAH! Is that what we want? Surprise? I don't know. I like surprise. The president all of a sudden rips your head off on the national TV, big surprise. See, there's the two types of death: the one you see coming, and the one you see as being invisible to you. What kind should this be? I don't know. Could be anything, is the beauty. I'm happy. The possibilities. It's a choice of freedom. Could be, um, uh, make you eat something. People like to eat, see other people eat. Maybe. Maybe you eat, uh, everything here on the desk. Fill up on, uh, papers, pen. Or maybe I just tighten up your tie real tight and you—or maybe you eat your tie.

(Bush puts Lehrer's tie in his mouth. Lehrer is passive.)

That's it. You eat your tie and, uh, that begins the choking procedure inside your throat and then, uh, as it descends your throat tightens up on the outside, so you are choking and being choked simul-tenuously. Go ahead. No, no, no, looks stupid. *(Bush takes the tie out of Lehrer's mouth.)* It's too, uh... but what am I gonna do? WHAT AM I GONNA DO? Surprise is good, but I DON'T KNOW. I CAN, I CAN ALMOST SAY IT, AND THEN...

Didn't like that little girl—the surprise she gave me, going in the water. Didn't like it. Didn't like that surprise and after it thought, "Well, that wasn't a surprise at all, just obviousnessness with her black dress, pearls, cigarette, and sorrowful song of course she's going to die." It was all just, uh, too much. Too much. I mean, if you're going to die, don't look like you're going to heh-heh die. Leave some mystery. The mystery shouldn't be in death, it should be in the lead-up to death. It's more satisfictional, mystery.

Except HERE. Don't like the mystery, how we're going to kill Jim Lehrer. Would like to revolve that mystery. Listen, the question is what's the best quality method to do it. Killing folks is interesting and it's necessary or something, and it just seems like the more interesting you make it the more necessary it will—I mean, this is America. We have always to do things interesting. Well, what's the most interesting way? Do you go to the theater, Mr. Lehrer?

LEHRER
What?

BUSH
Do you ever attend at the theater?

LEHRER
No... no I don't. Look, why don't we—

BUSH
Why is that?

LEHRER
I... I don't know. I just generally like to stay in, at home.

BUSH
You like that?

LEHRER
Sure. I like to sit and think about the news of the day. Like to think about it, then practice sort of saying it out loud.

BUSH
To yourself?

LEHRER
To myself, sure. See if it changes at all from how I think

about it to how I say it out loud.

BUSH
Does it change?

LEHRER
No, not much. I like to sit in my room with all the lights up very bright and think about it and then when I'm ready to say it, I turn up the lights a little more. Like I'm in the studio.

BUSH
Studio—that's like a theater?

LEHRER
Uh, no. No. It's a studio. And anyway I'm not in the studio, I'm in my room.

BUSH
With the lights up bright.

LEHRER
Yes.

BUSH
And, uh, just you there, alone? Saying the news?

LEHRER
Yes, alone. With my knives, of course.

BUSH
Knives. That's right. You have a collection.

LEHRER
Yes.

BUSH
Floor-to-ceiling, right?

LEHRER
Floor-to-ceiling, yes.

BUSH
See, now this is getting interesting. This could be it. Why is that? That you have that, uh, such an affliction for knives?

LEHRER
Well, I just like them, I... you know, in a world that's so, so... they're comforting. They're real.

BUSH
Real?

LEHRER
Sure. Or, anyway, they've got nothing to hide. Just bright and solid. As opposed to a gun, say, which could have any number of bullets—or anything, really—in it. You can't play Russian roulette with a knife. It is what it is.

BUSH
See, now this could be good. *(Bush opens a drawer on the side of Lehrer's desk and takes out a knife.)* Is this a knife?

LEHRER
Yes, that is the ritual Balinese kris dagger that I keep in my moderator's desk drawer at all times.

BUSH
Yeah, I knew about you having it there. It's not a stage knife? A prop? Like I used before?

LEHRER
No. Well, I suppose it is a stage knife in the sense that it is used in a ritual performance.

BUSH
So it is?

LEHRER
Well, yes, but it's on the stage that it becomes most real—and most dangerous. You see, in this ritual the young men of the village are forced into a trance and their knives, by their own hands, are turned against them by the evil witch Rangda.

BUSH
Maybe that was the problem with that other one. Not real. Maybe if I use this it will have meet our requirements. Do you, uh, what do you think? What do you think, Mr. Lehrer? About going straight to something real.

LEHRER
Well, the pillow was real. It's a real pillow.

BUSH
The pillow. Pillow's not real. Pillow's about sleep. Bring a pillow on stage everybody goes to sleep. Dreamland. No, this is real. And it's not rehearsal. Rehearsal's over. Rehearsal's over! REHEARSAL'S OVER.

(Lights dim. We hear an ominous drone. Bush circles around behind Lehrer, raises the knife above him, then at the last second pulls it back.)

I can't do it.

It's no good. I mean I feel like I'm in the middle-evil times or somewhere with this thing. Barbarian times. It's like if we just took off all our clothes up here. No sense of mystery, no finessement, no secret.

It's all wrong! We're just back to square, uh—first square. Square zero. So I've gotta, uh, got to just keep on with my story of what happened last night. But it's hard to keep—it's hard work. Hard work to talk. Hard work to make sense of my talking, to cause sense to be made in my talk. But it was revelationatory. I mean, you should've seen this play. They knew what they were—knew how to bring about a theater moment. I can't describe—can't speak it, it was so perfect. At the moment it came, this moment, then at the blackout, whole audience on their feet, hats in the air! Hats in the air! And they weren't cheering the blackout, no. No let's be clear, it's what comes up before the blackout that's worth yelling about. Hats in the air.

You should've seen this. This play. Like I say, though, it's hard—was hard work just to get there. Escape from dead mother, drive the ruined city, to the theater, the lobby, buy a ticket, find your seat, pay attention, keep focus, understand, intermission, freshen up, make it back, sit down, tug your pants, eat your peanut, clear your throat, focus again, concentrate, watch the actors, wait some more, then it comes, all connective with what came before, finally. The moment. Revelation.

But hard work—listen, we couldn't—didn't even know where the theater is. How we found it is took turns guessing which way to go. Through the smoke, come to a corner, the senator, from his dream state, from Dreamland, he takes a guess on the turn. Come to another intercession, I take a guess from Reality. So we alterstate the guessing: Dreamland, Reality, Dreamland, Reality. And we, uh, we arrive in bipartisaned manner. We made it work.

Finally turned the corner, there it was. Half the lights out, marquee sagging off the wall, smell of gas and burnt palm trees in their pots all around, coconuts gray, ashy. Fantastic place, however. Massive.

And purpose is—inside it I would find purpose. Didn't know it then, walking up the moldy marble steps. But inside was—I would find purpose. Not meaning, uh, necessarily. But purpose. I just can't talk and retriculate what—what... look, why don't I just—poison. I've got some cyanide back here and, uh, bourbon... glass of bourbon. *(Bush produces a glass, a bottle of bourbon, and a vial of powder from behind his lectern; puts some powder and bourbon in the glass.)* Just, uh, yeah, mix it up and, yeah. *(Sets the glass down in front of Lehrer.)* Just drink that. Just drink...

  (To the unseen light board operator:)

Bring 'em down. Slow.

  (Lights start to fade; music, wind sound effect up. Lehrer doesn't move.)

DRINK IT. DRINK IT.

  (Lehrer slowly raises the glass to his lips, considers. Then puts it down. Lights come up; music, wind stop.)

Mr. Lehrer? *(Pause.)* Look, why don't... just drink it.

LEHRER
I don't want to drink bourbon and cyanide.

BUSH
(Pause.) Yeah. I understand that. Wouldn't work to make you a co-collaborator. Wouldn't fly. There's got to be me

and—then you on the other side. Not one side together against itself. Wouldn't work. No drama.

AAAAA! I am out of ideas, ready to—and the story. The story of how to do this and why to do this is all scrambled-duh-dee in my mouth. You think I should give it up? Mr. Lehrer, you think I should unpursue the idea of your public murder?

LEHRER
I think we should move ahead with the debate.

BUSH
Move... move ahead. Good. Keep going, keep—struggle's everything. Everything is... just struggle. Go ahead. *(He drinks some bourbon from the bottle.)*

LEHRER
Very good. The question is for Senator Kerry. Two minutes, Senator Kerry.

You spoke to Congress in 1971, after you came back from Vietnam, and you said, quote, "How do you ask a man to be the last man to die for a mistake?"

Are Americans now dying in Iraq for a mistake?

KERRY
No, and they don't have to, providing we have the leadership that we put—that I'm offering. Nobody should die for a mistake. When we kill you, for example, it's my guarantee to you and the American people that we will do so with the full appearance of a sense of purpose. No mistake about it.

But as the president has just once again demonstrated, with

his surprise karate and dagger and cyanide, his approach in this matter is about nothing else but mistakes. Wrong directions.

And the story he wants to tell about the moment in the theater last night—there is no story. There is no story because there's no one to tell it. He can't tell it because of his... difficulties, and I can't tell it because I was asleep. It's all a fabulous muddle. Sure, I remember the little girl and her fall from the bridge, but not what I felt about it. I remember maybe that the theater was hot, that sweat had collected under my cuffs, that the chandeliers were dotted with flies. Random details. All that's important is that over the course of the play, while being entirely unconscious, I became every bit as convinced as the president that a way must be devised to do away with you, Jim. But how exactly did I become so convinced? It clearly had nothing to do with any experience in the waking world. So how? That is the mystery. And I'm claiming here tonight that that mystery is everything.

For it's not any story, it is the mystery, the secrets that a candidate for public office keeps that make him or her most attractive. America isn't interested in a candidate's phoniness, they're interested in what that phoniness conceals. Without secrets, a candidate has no depth, no richness, no meaning. A president should be like a very plain but ancient urn, sealed by unknown hands and set down among us so we might marvel at its invisible contents.

Unlike this president, I offer up no coherent narrative of why I think you should die, Jim. And so I am the more intriguing candidate. In my administration, Americans won't be dying for a mistake, they'll be dying for a mystery.

(Kerry walks down to Lehrer's desk, picks up the glass of cyanide and bourbon, and drinks it down.)

There's no mystery with this president. Only props.

(Kerry returns to his lectern.)

LEHRER
Mr. President, ninety sec—

BUSH
Now wait, that wasn't a prop, that was cyanide. I told you, he is a zom-bie. Card-waving member of the living dead. Of course he can drink it with—drink poison. And look, there's nothing—there's no intrigue-ary in him. No mystery. That's not the point. The bottom line, the bottom is he saw the same play I did. Saw the same play. And he came to the same concussion. Listen, sure, maybe he was asleep. But that's—there's your proof of the power of the show's moment. Able to permanate the the, uh—poke through the, uh, the veil of—crawl through the secret underbrush of the mist of sleep itself. Bust into Dreamland. He says he's steadfast. "Resolved." Then he says "wrong time, wrong place" for this death to occur. That's no kind of—the time is now. Tonight. I mean, here are the lights. Heat. Sound system. Stage. There's no other time. It's now. Sure we've got to do it right. The corrective way. Manner. *That's what I've been saying.* The reason to re-memorize what occurred last night is we learn from history. No matter how vaguely that history is dis-remembered, it can give a lesson. And we want to remember history so we can repeat it. Or we're, uh, doomed to uh, forget... it.

There is a way to kill people that does make, will make the whole world cheer. Hats in the air. I believe I saw a theatri-causation of that method last night. Here in this great city

of, uh, ruined city. DO YOU KNOW THE FEELING
OF WHICH I AM IN POSSESSION OF? BELIEVING
IN SOMETHING WHICH IS SECRET TO MYSELF
EVEN? Secrets are good. World can't run without secrets.
But, uh, I need to know this. *(To Kerry:)* AND I WILL
TELL IT.

Memory's just down there under the surface, I try to pull
it up it slips back down under, pull it up, slips down. Like
Slipisus with his boulder. But the deal in the reality of the
truth, the actuality is that my memory is, uh, it's perfect.
Perfect, uh, total, uh... everything. It's all in there. Here.
Where the problem is, is that how I talk to myself inside of
myself is, uh, how I talk outside. So there's disclarity. When
I tell, explain myself a memory, it is not clear. To me. And
it's painful. It hurts. Me. I mean the, uh, physicality of
my, uh, brain path as I attempt to attempt the memory
speaking. Through. But it's all in there. What happened.
JUST GOTTA MAKE IT TALK. FINISH IT.

Got to the place, walked up the steps, hello to everybody
in the lobby, the, uh, all the theater go-toers. Full house.
Happy people, just happy to be there, to have gotten
through. Milling in a big hot huddle, ladies fanning their
necks with old newspapers. In furs, all torn up, charred,
damp. Shake hands with people, senator still one hand with
the soda, employs the other. They got music pumping in
from a soggy speaker, violins, oboe. Pickpockets working
the crowd. More palm trees in pots. Mirrors, a red rug.
Marble walls, creamy purple—see, everything, it's in here!
And all of it, all these stuff, all here to make the theater and
its moment work for me! All connected!

So: wiped the ash off my shoulder, stood in the ticket line.
Senator went to fix his hair. I got the tickets to, uh, the
show was *Who is Afraid of Virginia Woolf?* By Ed Albee.

You know that show, Mr. Lehrer? About who Miss Woolf makes afraid?

LEHRER
Uh, no. No, I don't know that one.

BUSH
That's my—fantastic play. Classic. You don't?—you should see it.

LEHRER
Well, like I say, I don't get out much. Now—

BUSH
What's it about is these married people. George and, uh, Martha. And there's a, a, a—between Martha and George there's a, a big fight. And they, uh, fight, and, uh, combat—they are combative, and, uh, then they kill their kid. Only, see, it's not real, the uh, the uh, the uh, kid. They made it up. I don't mean to ruin the ending for everybody, but, uh, I guess I just did. They make up—they have this alternating reality with this, um, kid they made up, and then they have this big fight, and, uh, somewhere in there they—and like I say, it's all imagined in their minds, I mean on the interior of their minds, not, not what is ordinarily referred to as the exterior—at the end they kill him, this made-believe kid. And it's often very sad. That moment of killing. But, uh, uh, now this is the moment that I am trying to, uh, say. This is what's of import. Both the fact that it happened and also now that I will describe it as happened, how it happened. Okay, uh... here's what it was. My opponent and I in the front row. Peanuts. Beer. Here's what it was.

(Pause. Long, odd pause.)

LEHRER

Mr. President... *(Pause.)* That's ninety seconds, Mr. President.

BUSH

Just one of my pauses...

LEHRER

I'm sorry, Mr. President...

KERRY

Jim, can I, uh—

LEHRER

Yes, yes; thirty seconds, Senator.

KERRY

Thank you, Jim. "Who is afraid of Virginia Woolf?" Well, that's certainly, I'm sure, a fine question for the waking members of the theatrical community, like Mr. Albee, to ask, and I'm sure Mr. Albee—being a bright-eyed, alert, and, above all, conscious playwright—I'm sure Mr. Albee answers the pressing question of his title. And now, perhaps, the president will now argue that the answer to the question regarding Ms. Woolf is somehow tied to the effectiveness of his "theatrical moment" and thus hard fastened to his conviction that the only thing to do with your life, Jim, is to do away with it as entertainingly as possible, this evening. Well, the president is free to pluck whatever cherries of significance he likes from Mr. Albee's play or any play, but in my experience the only thing the theater offers consistently, and deliciously so, is sleep. Down through the ages, through all its genres and periods, the power to persuade the minds of select audience members to first dim, then darken, has been the theater's only mainstay. The theater claims many powers, but its power to induce slumber is the only one we can be certain of and the only one of real value. To hell with what's on the stage, with any "theater moment." What else is there but that warm bed of the audience—that bed most lush to curl within and let fall one's chin and lashes, knowing nothing of the world but the tug of the beer stein dangling from the small finger on one's drooping hand. Who among us would require more? Go to sleep. Go to sleep...

LEHRER
Mr. President—

BUSH
Yeah, no response, just go onto the next, uh, the next—

LEHRER
All right. Mr. President, this is the last—

BUSH
They did a real kid.

LEHRER
Mr. President, I haven't asked the question.

BUSH
Doesn't matter. They did a real kid. An actual, uh, a baby. That was the twist, the, uh, the moment. It was real. And they killed it in reality. Brought it out in a green blanket, crying, snot down its face. There in the crumblings of that broken-down stage with all the dark and disease of the city all around outside. George and Martha killed a baby. And it was, uh, was dead. There was blood, and, uh, pieces of... they used razor blades. Very slowly, with music, George—the actor playing George cut into the—around the chest, the lungs. And the Martha actor knelt by to wipe away the, uh—they had a light aimed specially on the razor so

it would glinter. And Martha, all the time, uh, she didn't want to do it. So she's uh, saying, "no George, no George" but all the time still helping wipe away the uh, um, yeah. The play goes on during all this, the cutting and wiping, just the end lines, until the end and I think there is where it did die. Timed with the final lines. And, uh, right before it died, turned its head, full head of hair, looked right at me—out of everybody—and gave out the softest scream. Very soft. And that was it. And that was the only time that night and this I was able to stop hearing my mother's scream. That was it. Great theater moment. That was it. *(Pause.)* But that's not it. Because you still don't—I can tell I have not—I still can't say, describe, how they did it. It was so—it was such a high production standard—the light, music—that, uh, like I say: hats in the air. Everybody on their feet. And look, people weren't just cheering the death of a baby. It was everything that went before, just very high production standard. And what came after: fade to black. With music.

(Lights begin to fade; music and wind sound effect begin.)

That was the clincher, the blackout. That's always the way: descent, fade into total darkness. That's the moment. Whatever the moment is that comes before, killing a kid, whatever, that's not the moment. The moment is the blackness. And it's indiffer-ence to the moment or prior moments before. That's when—you get your revelation then: nothing matters. And the more extra something feels like it matters before the blackout, the more big the revelation that it doesn't matter when the blackout occurs. When it's upon you. When you're in it. And that's our duty in this world. To make, make it feel like it matters up onto the point we find out it doesn't. Matter.

(Lights up; music and wind stop.)

But as to the manner. How did—how was it done? I remember but cannot say, cannot inarticulate it to myself.

I see the dead infant. I hear the audience cheer. I see hats flying. I have described the blackout. But what came before? The razor, music, sure—but the finer details, the staging-craft. It is encumbered upon me as the nation's leader to understand how it is to be done. There should be in the final place of things no secrets from me. Not in the city. Not in my mind. I should know the proper execution of how to do away with you. How to do it so there is a pleasantness in how... so it is acceptable. To all people. So it's *universal*, uh, *elemental*, I should know—

(Bush pulls out a can of gasoline from behind his lectern.)

Fire. Fire. OKAY, BIG FINISH HERE. BIG FIRE. BIG SPECTACULAR.

(He rushes over to Lehrer and pours gas over him. Takes out a lighter, lights it, approaches Lehrer. Stops. Pause.)

But... but if I make you on fire, uh, how to get the blackout? Can't have a decent blackout with a someone burning in the middle of the stage. That won't... don't see how that could—AAAAAGH!

(Bush pours the rest of the gas on himself. Flicks open the lighter. Then closes it.)

LEHRER
All right, that brings us to closing statements. And, again, as determined by a coin toss, President Bush, you go first, and you have two minutes.

BUSH

Mr. Lehrer, help me. What am I—what am I doing, don't know. Can't even do this—make an end of myself. I explained it to myself why to do it, but I misclarified the explanation. So, uh... yeah.

(Pause.)

Mr. Lehrer, um... maybe you notice sometimes, uh, I pause in my speaking? In my—*(Pause.)* What's happening in there maybe you are thinking. In that pause. *(Pause.)* Well, things maybe, uh, sometimes I think inside that pause there is just one thing happening. And that's nothing. Nothing is in that pause. No decision or misdecision. No mistakes, corrections. No life. No death, secrets, sleep. Just nothing. And I go away in there. And being away in nothing how am I—who is to do away with me? Not me. Not him. Not you. Who is to do the doing away of people like me? Who have—who at times are possessioned of nothing-ness. Who can hide away into nothing-ness. I am forever eternal and long-lasting.

But still have failed, Mr. Lehrer. Tonight. I tell you it's a difficult job making people applause for the death of an innocent person. Hard work making people clap the death of a kid, baby, or respected newscaster. Mostly because they just don't care. I mean haven't we all, everybody, come to this same—where it's just hard work to remember every day why it's of an importance to applaud the death of innocent lives? That enthusiasm is necessary to—for us to get the job done. Me and, uh, everybody watching me. I need your support. In the end it's the audience makes the moment work. I mean, there's people being killed now. Ripped open kids. Anybody clapping? See, that's my difficulty. How am I to get enthusiastical approval for your murder when there's this indiffer-ence?

Anyway, vote for me.

LEHRER
Senator Kerry, two minutes.

KERRY
Thank you, Jim, very much.

Thank you very much to the university, again.

Thank you, Mr. President.

My fellow Americans, I just had the weirdest dream. Only I can't remember what it was now. I remember you were all in it and we were going somewhere. Or someone was coming over to visit, or something. I don't remember. I don't remember.

LEHRER
And that ends tonight's debate. A reminder, the second presidential debate will be a week from tomorrow, October 8th, from Washington University in St. Louis. Charles Gibson of ABC News will moderate a town hall-type event. Then, on October 13th, from Arizona State University in Tempe, Bob Schieffer of CBS News will moderate an exchange on domestic policy that will be similar in format to tonight's.

For now, thank you, Senator Kerry, President Bush. From Coral Gables, Florida, I'm Jim Lehrer. Thank you and good night.

(Lehrer is still while he waits for the cameras to go off, then gathers up his papers, rises to go.)

LEHRER
Yes, Mr. President. We're finished here.

BUSH
Cameras turned off?

LEHRER
I imagine so.

BUSH
Everybody gone?

LEHRER
Mm. Goodbye, Mr. President. Senator.

BUSH
Wait.

LEHRER
Yes?

BUSH
Where you going?

LEHRER
Just back to my hotel room. Thought I'd practice the news for a few hours before my flight.

BUSH
Thinkin' it and then sayin' it?

LEHRER
Yes, that's what I do. *(Pause. Lehrer picks up the kris knife and hands it to Bush.)* You know, sir, I understand how hard your job can be at times. And to be frank, you seem a little down. So let me offer you this as a, I don't know, a

souvenir of our evening. It's a beautiful knife, which has personally brought me much comfort in my contemplation of it. It is, as you've noted, quite real. Perhaps outside the scrutiny of an audience it will take on that mystery you felt it lacked.

Gentlemen.

(Lehrer exits. Pause.)

BUSH
He forgot his knife.

Why would he...

I better, uh, better go give it to him. Go find his room. *(To Kerry:)* You stay here. Take a nap. Uh, yeah...

(Bush exits.)

KERRY
Oh, here's what it was. I remember now. We were all here, in this room. Only the cameras had been turned off, and all of you had gone, and there was no one here but me. Like now. And I was talking, like now, to no one, because everybody had left—the president was off doing something offstage, the debate was over, everyone had gone. So I was talking to—who was I talking to? And it occurred to me that the dream had just begun, but without me, somewhere out there. And the president was in it, and all of you, and he was doing something offstage— maybe with a knife, maybe with his bare hands, maybe with fire, water, it didn't matter what or how. It was just he was doing it, and we couldn't quite see what it was, especially me. *(Lights begin to go out, as though being shut off by someone backstage.)* And I couldn't remember this

dream. And I was talking to no one. Like now. Who am I talking to? There is no one to listen. There is no one here. It is, to me *(Blackout.)* heaven.

END

JIM LEHRER
AND **THE THEATER**
AND **ITS DOUBLE**
AND **JIM LEHRER'S DOUBLE**

"There is a knife which I do not forget. But it is a knife which is halfway into dreams, which I keep inside myself, which I do not allow to come to the frontier of the lucid senses."

— *Antonin Artaud*

Jim Lehrer and the Theater and Its Double and Jim Lehrer's Double was first produced in 2017 by Theater Oobleck at the Chopin Theater in Chicago with the following cast:

Jim Lehrer	Colm O'Reilly
Jim Lehrer (II)	Brian Shaw

CHARACTERS:
Jim Lehrer

SETTING:
The small sitting room just off the foyer of the retired Jim Lehrer's spacious and indifferently-furnished DC suburban home. Two chairs with a small table between. An area rug.

NOTES:
The staging should make a point of having no logic to where the actors' exits take them, or where their entrances are from. The chairs and table should seem to bob in a black space, outside of which there is no sensible architecture. The exit/entrance to the front door, e.g., is off one way at one time, another way at another time.

In the opening monologue in particular, and anywhere else either Lehrer or his double speaks alone, the actor should address no one but himself, but all the while look at a point perhaps just to the side of the audience, or just above their heads, as though there were a camera there. Not breaking the fourth wall, in other words, but doing something like. Breaking the 3 and ¾'s wall, maybe. Lehrer's tone, at the top, is the one he used on his broadcasts, or while moderating presidential debates.

A slash (/) indicates that the next speaker's line overlaps the first, breaking in at that point in the sentence.

(In the dark, we hear a doorbell ring. At lights up, Jim Lehrer is seated next to a table, on which is a cup of tea and a single-sheet questionnaire.)

JIM LEHRER

Good evening, from the small sitting room just off the foyer at the entrance of my spacious and indifferently-furnished DC suburban home, I'm Jim Lehrer, formerly of the PBS NewsHour, and tonight...

(Pauses. Considers the questionnaire. Picks it up and looks it over. Puts it down. Wants to get this right.)

Good evening, from the small sitting room just off the foyer at the entrance of my spacious and casually-furnished DC suburban home, I'm Jim Lehrer, of the PBS NewsHour, retired. And tonight in a slight break from...

(Pauses. Rewinds.)

...DCsuburbanhomeI'mJimLehrerofthePBSNewsHour... and tonight, in an exciting break from my routine of thinking the news of my uneventful late-evening hours and then saying the news of my uneventful late-evening hours, in a departure from my normal evening habit of reporting to myself the rundown of the news of my day to myself, alone, from either my place-setting at the dinner table or alone at my desk in the den—tonight I think on the news of my life and report on the news of my life from this small sitting room just off the foyer at the entrance to my home. This change in usual location was brought about by the ringing of my doorbell just moments ago, a ringing that had me going to the door, opening it, and greeting a pleasant but fairly nondescript woman who was conducting a poll, or rather, working for an established polling firm, going door-to-door—to all of my neighbors

I'm assuming, and beyond my neighbors to areas unfamiliar to me—going door-to-door with a poll on our imminent village council election. She asked if I would be willing to take a moment to fill out this poll while she canvassed the area. I agreed to this, and she said she would be back in a little while. And rather than return to my place-setting at the dinner table, or go, as is my usual habit, to the desk in my den, or my bedroom, or to the room which houses my floor-to-ceiling collection of rare knives—rather than go to any of these places to report on the events of my life, I was so thrilled, I thought: Why not get started right here and now, here, near the door where I received the poll in this, its paper form.

(He looks at the poll.)

We're going to take a short break now, so I can take a moment to look over the poll and settle myself down before diving in and completing the poll the best I can.

(Waits a second for his imagined camera to go dark, then relaxes, as though off the air now. Sets the poll down and studies it, sipping his tea. Checks his breast pocket for a pen. No luck. Gets up and exits. After a long moment comes back with the stub of a pencil. Sits and looks over the poll. Sips tea. Readies himself, then addresses the camera point again.)

Okay, we're back. Again, this is Jim Lehrer formerly of the PBS NewsHour, former presidential debate moderator, reporting tonight from the sitting room near the front door of my modestly appointed DC suburban home. It's a late summer evening, and an uncharacteristically chilly one. Outside, in the darkness, a friendless wind blows, as a thick mist dulls the entire sky and curls through my neighborhood's lanes and cul-de-sacs.

To recap my main story:

I've received a poll this evening that asks questions and seeks my opinions—my "takes"—on the two candidates in the election for the head of our village council. I'm champing at the bit to go through these questions, from the beginning, the "top," answering each of them honestly. Honesty is important to me. In my professional life, I tried to be honest when speaking to the cameras, and in retirement, I try now, in my day-to-day description of events to myself, to speak true, when there are no cameras anymore. I am aware that I am speaking—reporting—only to myself, that I am talking only to myself, that there is no one else here, but nevertheless, I do my utmost to be true and factual in my *reportage*. Whether this is the case for all people in the world, if all people are truthful both in their public lives and when talking to themselves, I cannot say, but I would hope it to be so.

I am a lonely man these days, a fallen leaf trying to make my peace with the cold skin of a sullen earth, and I've come to think of my truthfulness as a sort of companion. My one companion is my honesty.

The only writing implement I was able to find without hunting through the whole house was this pencil stub, next to my to-do list on the parson's table by the front door. I don't do much writing currently, mostly just my usual thinking of the news of my day and speaking the news of my day, so I have little need for pencils or pens. This will have to do.

At this time, I'm eager to read and then answer the first question.

The first question of this poll regarding the candidates

in the council election is: On a scale of one to ten with one being the lowest and ten being the highest, how honest would you rate (and here is named the Republican nominee) to be?

(A pained pause.)

Because I haven't considered this question much in my life, I hesitate to answer. I simply don't think much on the honesty or dishonesty of other people, or candidates for political office, as I am focused so much in my moment-to-moment life on whether or not I am an honest person. I have scrutinized no one but myself in this regard.

And look.

There is nowhere on the form to plead ignorance. It is almost as if I am being compelled to tell an untruth.

I had hopes for this activity. But now find myself, here at the outset, in a sort of despair. Ready to crumple up this poll, and return to the usual habits of my evening. But it is a rare event, these days, for me to have engagement of any sort with... what's out there. This poll is my slender tether to the world. I *will* complete it. Adrenaline is assaulting the dug-in encampment of my heart.

I go on to the next question on the form. Question number two. I will return to the first question, which remains unanswered, at a later point.

(Here, and perhaps other places, Lehrer turns 45 degrees or so, switching camera points.)

As a side note, it is remarkable to me that though I need to understand language to *take* this poll, no language is required of me to *respond.* I only need to check a box to make comprehendible my heretofore concealed opinions.

(Switching back to the main camera.)

In any case, the second question is: On a scale of one to ten with one being the lowest and ten being the highest, how honest would you rate (and here is named the Democratic nominee) to be?

(Here he lets out a strange cry of anguish—a strongly repressed one, as from a dog who's whipped and then ordered not to bark.)

Aaurhrrr.

This question, the second question, is almost a perfect mirror of the first. It probes an empty space, seeking thoughts of mine that don't exist. Again: I have not considered the truthfulness of any candidate. And to ask me to do so now is to ask that I plunge into an impenetrable forest of unformed thought and guess-work.

Maybe if I had something other than tea to refresh myself I would find the heart to continue. A cracker, perhaps. A dish of nuts. A packet of dried fruit. Let's pause for a short while as I go to the kitchen and pantry in search of one or more of these items.

(He exits.)

(A second Jim Lehrer enters. Let's call him Jim Lehrer II. He wears a suit and tie much the same as Jim Lehrer's, but it's ripped and bloodied and muddied. His face and exposed skin are bruised and scratched and smudged with dirt. He is worried that he's being followed. He sits in

*the second chair. Picks up the mug of tea and sniffs it.
Puts it down. Takes up the pencil stub, looks it over, puts
it down. Slides the poll over and looks it over. Addresses
the air, nobody, but, again, to a specific point, as though
there were a camera, just off.)*

JIM LEHRER II

Good evening, I'm Jim Lehrer, reporting tonight from the
small sitting room just off the foyer at the entrance of my
DC suburban home, somewhat quietly, as I have reason
to believe a large group of angry people is in search of me,
and I don't want to make much noise.

I've just returned from the premiere of the light, topical
play I authored for a local amateur theatrical company.
It was not well received. The audience exhibited an
irritation through the initial scenes, an irritation which
devolved in time into an odd indignation, finally growing
to an inexplicable, even surreal, fury. All became a chaos
of bizarre incident. At curtain's close, there were angry
chants, and a sort of rage-fueled improvised stomping-
dance. I remember, in particular, one man shredding his
program, like a hawk does a rodent's viscera. Such heat in
his eyes: as though it were not a mere informational record
of my play and its participants, but *the play itself* he would
destroy.

What offense my slight entertainment gave, or how it
produced such a strange response, I can't guess. Perhaps
the audience's reaction was a reflection of the mood of our
village council election season, which has coaxed forth
a plague-fever of acrimony along all points of our small
suburb's political continuum. Or perhaps we have entered
a period where the intention of a play and its ultimate
reception by the public are two things entirely, infinitely,
divorced. But I don't wish to speculate. I don't know

what's true. The bottom line is, my play, at its conclusion, inspired the audience to charge backstage and threaten me, the playwright, with violence. At first it was more a game, in the vein of a display-strut prior to a mating selection combat: they feinted and growled, with winks and grimaces while advancing and retreating, wagging their fingers, and jutting their chins. But soon the blood was in their face, and seizing up their fists they fell forward as one. It was all so suddenly Real. Luckily, I suffered only some minor injuries, being able to defend myself, in part, with the hunting knife I habitually carry when attending any public entertainment.

(He produces a hunting knife and puts it on the table.)

I fled from my audience through the fields of grass and rushes that grow untended behind the theater. Inside a mist rotted through with the diseased-tissue gleam of a quarter moon, I came upon a creek I am familiar with, and knowing that it runs near to my home, I followed it here, scrambling its cold water, scraping my ankles on its sharp stones, my thighs scourged by the nettles that overhung its banks. The sound of lost pigs in the distance.

Whither my dreams, I sang.

I must warn the other Jim Lehrer of this household of the mob that has likely tracked me to this address. I've already locked the front door and turned off the porch light—the other Jim Lehrer may have further ideas on how best to secure the property.

(He takes out his phone.)

I would call the police but my phone was soaked through when I stumbled in the creek, and has gone dead.

I've noticed Jim's tea here, now lukewarm. It is unusual for him to sit and report on the news of his day from here in the sitting room off the foyer, but I see here this poll on the imminent election. I can only assume this was recently given him to fill out and he thought best to work on it here, on location, close to our front door, where he would have received it.

I am supposing that he's currently in the kitchen and pantry, looking for a snack. I'll seek him there, in the kitchen, to remind him of the fact of my existence—a fact which he invariably forgets.

I am in a sanity-endangering panic.

> (He exits. The first Jim Lehrer returns. He has a dish of nuts.)

JIM LEHRER
We're back. I'm Jim Lehrer. I took several wrong turns on my way to the kitchen, and as a result was half-lost for a time in my own home. But in the end, I did find it, the kitchen, and was able to pour for myself this dish of almonds.

> (He eats one, taking his time.)

Fortified, I now return to the questions of this troublesome poll. Question number three.

> (He sees the hunting knife Jim Lehrer II left. Picks it up.)

In an unusual development, I've just now discovered a fair-sized hunting knife here on the small table in my sitting room. An ordinary Hoffman Richter Tactical, partially serrated, folding blade. It appears it was recently used, there being some still tacky blood on the bevel, and traces of flesh or sinew pooled here near the bolster.

(Pause. He listens.)

Is someone there?

If someone is there, be aware I am armed with the very knife that you, yourself, left here on my table. If this is not your knife, be aware I have the knife left by somebody else, a second intruder, perhaps unknown to yourself, intruder number one. If that second intruder is now listening, they should be cognizant as well of my readiness to defend myself—with the knife that belongs to one or the other of you.

In a moment I'm going to stand and go in search of you. Whether you be one or more.

(He stands. Makes to go.)

Though I exit now to face a possible antagonist, I feel it is the better part of caution to fold this knife's blade away, to guard against pricking myself in the darkness as I wander.

(Folds knife, exits. Jim Lehrer II enters, blowing on a mug of bouillon. Sits.)

JIM LEHRER II

We're back. Jim Lehrer reporting. I have been all over the house, and while I believe I heard my counterpart at times, moving about, I was unable to locate him. I got a little spooked and so returned here, stopping by the kitchen first to heat up this comforting mug of bouillon. And just now this instant I've just noticed that my knife—which I left here—is missing. I will now speak somewhat louder.

WHO TOOK MY KNIFE? MR. LEHRER?

(Quietly.) I don't think it would have been him. He is a great *aficionado* of knives, my counterpart, with a very impressive collection of rare and unusual blades. My unremarkable hunting knife would've held no interest for him.

WHO TOOK THE KNIFE?

> *(A sound is heard, off. Distant, echoing. Perhaps a moan, or retreating footsteps, a creak, a flutter, or a single note, sung, and its echo.)*

WHO IS THERE?

> *(He listens for any response. There's none.)*

If I go back to the kitchen, I might then find a sharp implement of some sort with which to defend myself.

> *(As he goes out, away from the direction of the sound:)*

MR. LEHRER. JIM. IT'S ME. JIM LEHRER. I'VE RETURNED FROM THE THEATER.

> *(He's gone. Jim Lehrer enters, still holding the hunting knife.)*

JIM LEHRER
I'm Jim Lehrer, formerly of the PBS NewsHour, and someone is calling my name. Someone who, oddly, sounds like myself.

> *(Sees the mug of bouillon, sniffs it.)*

And someone who is leaving behind knives, and bouillon.

Though it is regrettable when the reporter, himself, becomes the story, I confess—now that it is happening—I am tickled by the prospect.

(Jim exits, carrying the bouillon and the knife. Jim II enters, with a cleaver, sucking his hand.)

JIM LEHRER II
Mmmmofthat smarts. I just nicked the back of my hand on something back there. Mmmmouch.

JIM!

(Jim II exits. No pause, Jim enters, drinking the bouillon, finishes it off and sets the empty mug on the table. He exits. Jim II enters, with a draft of his play, unbound, bedecked with post-its and fluttering, paper-clipped note scraps. One of his shoes is missing.)

JIM LEHRER II
I haven't found Mr. Lehrer, but I found this next to the recliner in the den. The rehearsal draft of my play. I didn't put it there, by the recliner, in the magazine cradle. I imagine that was Jim. I hope he liked what he read.

Here's my mug, emptied.

(Again, a sound, distant, but from elsewhere. Perhaps the same sound as before, or not.)

JIM? JIM WHERE ARE YOU?

(Goes in search of him, in the direction of the sound this time, leaving the rough draft on the table. We hear Jim

singing off in the distance, Purcell's "Cold Genius".)

JIM LEHRER
What Power art thou,
Who from below,
Hast made me rise,
Unwillingly and slow,
From beds of everlasting snow!

(He's entered by now, and is eating a popsicle.)

That's a song about when you're wanting to freeze to death in the snow, but then some under-worldly force compels you to save yourself. It's here on the strayed page of a document I was reading in the den, a page I found on the dark hall floor on my way back from the kitchen.

And here's the rest of it. What I was reading before I was given this poll. Who has come to visit?

I found this frozen treat in the rear of the freezer.

I like it.

But it's going to later make me thirsty.

(He puts what's left of the popsicle—if anything—into the empty mug. Exiting:)

Who has come?

(Jim II enters, still with cleaver. Sucking his hand again.)

JIM LEHRER II
I heard singing. My hand was caught again on something back there is when I heard it. A singing which may have

been Jim Lehrer's, or an intruder's. Those are the two possibilities this evening, and I'll be thinking and reporting on them as things develop.

My panic is accumulating mass, as a dead body does when thrown from a high turret. It plummets through me, my panic, with increasing velocity, as I, on some swept ground below, watch it missile towards my head, enlarging on its approach.

(Again, a distant sound, from somewhere else in the house. Jim II steps towards it.)

What. What was that? Singing again?

(Jim enters, from a place other than where the noise came.)

JIM LEHRER
No one is singing.

JIM LEHRER II
(A little startled.) Oh, good evening, Jim. Thank goodness.

(Long pause.)

JIM LEHRER
Good evening.

(Pause.)

I don't know who this is.

(To Jim II:) Who are you?

JIM LEHRER II
During my times of absence—out shopping my plays, or trying to write at the café—it's Mr. Lehrer's habit to forget that I exist.

I'm Jim Lehrer.

JIM LEHRER
I'm Jim Lehrer.

JIM LEHRER II
I'm Jim Lehrer.

JIM LEHRER
I don't remember there being another Jim Lehrer. And I don't remember being a forgetful person.

JIM LEHRER II
There really is no satisfying explanation for it, but the fact is he does—you do—forget me. I have my theory as to why.

JIM LEHRER
I would be interested in hearing that theory.

JIM LEHRER II
He is attached to his loneliness. Many times, I have heard you, Jim Lehrer, say "Loneliness is my one companion." Having another Jim Lehrer in the house, you quit that Loneliness. With some regret.

He forgets me, from time to time, to welcome Loneliness back.

JIM LEHRER
No, see, I don't say that Loneliness is my one companion,

I say Honesty. Honesty is my one companion.

JIM LEHRER II
Oh. Is that true? I must have misremembered. I apologize.

JIM LEHRER
Strange that someone who claims to be myself should not remember what it is I often say.

JIM LEHRER II
Not so strange. The both of us are forgetful of things these days.

JIM LEHRER
Yes, well, in any case, I hardly think it plausible that I would bleep out the knowledge that I live in the same house with another man named Jim Lehrer, and that.

(Beat.)

Oh.

(Laughs, happily.)

It took me a moment, a minute or two, but I now remember that I do, in fact, live in the same house with another man named Jim Lehrer. Like a candle's flame abides with its pale shadow. This second Jim Lehrer is not and has never been a successful news anchor for the Public Broadcasting Service, or any other national network. He is a playwright, and so has never had a consequential relationship to the actual world or its motions.

Welcome home, Mr. Lehrer.

JIM LEHRER II

Thank you.

JIM LEHRER

I am so happy it's you, and not some unknown person.

JIM LEHRER II

I feel the same of you.

JIM LEHRER

Let's hear about the evening. Were you at a—what's the term—a rehearsal?

JIM LEHRER II

No, but I need to warn you. A play of mine premiered this evening.

JIM LEHRER

Well, that's not reason for warning. That's cause for congratulations. If you were not sucking on your hand I would shake it.

JIM LEHRER II

I'm sorry. I cut myself on something.

JIM LEHRER

Are you going to be all right?

JIM LEHRER II

Oh, no. It's fine.

JIM LEHRER

Let me have a look.

> (He takes Jim II's hand and examines the minuscule nick with concern.)

Oh, yes. I see it there. Did you nick it on this rather run-of-the-mill cleaver of yours?

JIM LEHRER II
No, I don't think so.

(Jim Lehrer kisses it.)

JIM LEHRER
All better now.

JIM LEHRER II
Thank you. That really worked. Your kissing it.

JIM LEHRER
Are we friends? Do we get along?

JIM LEHRER II
Oh, yes. For some time.

JIM LEHRER
How long for?

JIM LEHRER II
I think, well, at least since your retirement.

JIM LEHRER
Since the days of my speaking to the entire nation, the entire world.

JIM LEHRER II
Sure.

JIM LEHRER
Being on a stage with presidents and their challengers.

JIM LEHRER II
At least since. Yes.

JIM LEHRER
Asking *them* the questions. Polling *them*. Oh, what a time, that was a time. Yes?

JIM LEHRER II
Yes it was.

JIM LEHRER
And now you, you're on a stage. A theatrical premiere. Why wasn't I invited to your entertainment?

JIM LEHRER II
I mentioned it but you preferred to stay at home. With your Loneliness and your collection of knives.

JIM LEHRER
My. A theatrical premiere! Does this pile of papers here on the table have anything to do with that?

JIM LEHRER II
That's an early draft of my play. Did you read it?

JIM LEHRER
I did.

JIM LEHRER II
And what did Jim Lehrer think of Jim Lehrer's play?

JIM LEHRER
How much does it match with the current version? Tonight's version?

JIM LEHRER II
Oh, they're quite different in some essential ways.

JIM LEHRER
I wish I had been there this evening. In the audience. I'm honestly proud of you. My double. My "twin."

JIM LEHRER II
Well, thank you. But, no, I'm glad you weren't there.

JIM LEHRER
Oh?

JIM LEHRER II
It did not go well, and as a result our home may be invaded.

JIM LEHRER
Aren't twins often evil? Isn't that something I heard?

JIM LEHRER II
It's often the way in literature and film and television, yes. "The Evil Twin."

JIM LEHRER
But we're not, either of us, that way.

JIM LEHRER II
Oh, no.

JIM LEHRER
Unless maybe you're not my twin. That would be a mean trick on your part.

JIM LEHRER II
No, no trick. I'm Jim Lehrer.

JIM LEHRER
As am I. I wonder how I'd feel if you weren't, though.

JIM LEHRER II
How's that?

JIM LEHRER
It would be so strange.

JIM LEHRER II
If I weren't you?

JIM LEHRER
If someone who looked and sounded so exactly like myself, as you do, turned out to be not myself.

JIM LEHRER II
Oh.

JIM LEHRER
How would I feel about that?

JIM LEHRER II
It would be a terror. Like looking in a mirror and seeing someone else looking back.

JIM LEHRER
Yes. Fortunately, mirrors don't work that way, do they?

JIM LEHRER II
No, I don't believe so.

JIM LEHRER
They don't monkey with the old switcheroo.

JIM LEHRER II
No.

JIM LEHRER
Well let me tell you my happy news. I've been given a poll to complete.

JIM LEHRER II
Oh, yes.

JIM LEHRER
A woman came to the door—*right up to the door*—rang the bell, I opened up, and she handed it to me. Our fingers touched.

JIM LEHRER II
You've passed over the first two questions, I noticed.

JIM LEHRER
Right to the door.

JIM LEHRER II
And haven't gotten to the others yet.

JIM LEHRER
That's right. It's very difficult. And she's coming back. She'll ring soon. Would you like an almond?

JIM LEHRER II
No, I'd better not.

JIM LEHRER
When she rings the bell, then we'll let her in. That's how I managed it the first time.

JIM LEHRER II
Oh, no, that's wrong.

JIM LEHRER
Wrong?

JIM LEHRER II
We need to disconnect the ringer. And we need to stay away from the door.

JIM LEHRER
Oh, yes. You said something about an invasion. Who is invading?

JIM LEHRER II
The audience from my play this evening.

JIM LEHRER
Is that ordinary?

JIM LEHRER II
That an audience, flush with some contagion of the stage, should stalk a playwright to his home?

JIM LEHRER
Oh, dear.

JIM LEHRER II
Not in my experience, no.

JIM LEHRER
Oh, dear.

JIM LEHRER II
But this is my first produced work, I should mention.

JIM LEHRER
Is that a fact. Well double congratulations, then. "Twin" congratulations.

JIM LEHRER II
I don't feel I am to be congratulated.

JIM LEHRER
But your play... story... provoked such a vigorous response. How ever did it do that?

JIM LEHRER II
The fact is, I don't know. But there is. There is this: a minute or so into the first scene, there was a problem with the old grid. Something went wrong. From the wings, hunched on my stool, I heard a muffled scraping and the Fresnels and PAR cans suddenly slipped their focus and became aimed straight down.

JIM LEHRER
Straight down.

JIM LEHRER II
It created an unusual effect. The actors were a-swim upstream in a vertical flood of light, and so had no shadow, any of them.

JIM LEHRER
No shadow.

JIM LEHRER II
Like in a boxing ring. Yes. *(He remembers now.)* That's when things began to go wrong. The audience began, then, to turn. A cough and grumble from someone near the back wall, and the discontent spread like a flaming slick over every row. And I, myself, was not immune. I felt

my play become Not Me. Violent and Strange and in no way a reflection of myself. How is that possible? Even in dreams I've not lost the Who of myself. The recognition. But tonight, under those lights, the audience curiously aroused, the play went forward. And it was.

(Pause.)

It became.

(Pause.)

JIM LEHRER
What? What did it become?

JIM LEHRER II
An opening. Into the permissible. All urges, all lusts, all fears and cruelties. Permissible.

JIM LEHRER
Because of this lighting effect?

JIM LEHRER II
I don't know. It's all a fog.

JIM LEHRER
There were bright lights and all that in my newscasts and debates.

JIM LEHRER II
Of course.

JIM LEHRER
We never had much of a problem.

JIM LEHRER II
No.

JIM LEHRER
Listen, I need help with this poll.

JIM LEHRER II
I think we should call the police.

JIM LEHRER
Because of, oh, because of your audience. You know, I read these pages of yours / and I

JIM LEHRER II
Where is your phone?

JIM LEHRER
My phone? I don't use it much.

JIM LEHRER II
You have one, though. We're on the same plan. A two-for-one deal.

JIM LEHRER
It could be anywhere in the house. Where is your phone?

JIM LEHRER II
I drenched it in the creek. It won't turn on.

JIM LEHRER
I've heard or read that if you put a wet phone in rice or cat litter it fixes things somehow. We have some rice in the pantry.

JIM LEHRER II
Okay. Why don't we go there and get a bowl of it.

JIM LEHRER
Oh, no. I should stay here and work on this poll and wait for the pollster. You go ahead.

(*Pause. Jim II goes to exit, teeters on the brink, thinks better of it.*)

JIM LEHRER II
I'd rather we now stay together. Let's just go quickly, the both of us, to the pantry.

JIM LEHRER
(*Working on the poll.*) It's just so very difficult. You're a writer. What do you think of these questions?

JIM LEHRER II
I don't write polls.

JIM LEHRER
You don't? What do you write?

JIM LEHRER II
Well, plays. Like tonight's.

JIM LEHRER
But no polls. You never tried your hand.

JIM LEHRER II
I can take another look if you like.

JIM LEHRER
I would appreciate.

(*Hands him the poll. As Jim II looks it over, Jim picks up the play draft.*)

You say your play event tonight was vastly different from this version that I read?

JIM LEHRER II
All plays divorce themselves from their scripts.

JIM LEHRER
Well, why a script in the first place, then? If it's just going to wind up in a divorce?

JIM LEHRER II
The idea is that in that divorce, in that space of difference between the written word and the performed, is where the success or failure of a play emerges.

JIM LEHRER
Well. I once read from a script. Reporting the news of the day. And there was no divorce. Read the script silently to myself, thought about it, read it quietly to myself, and then read it out loud to the country and world. No divorce. A perfect match, script and performance.

JIM LEHRER II
You were very good at what you did.

JIM LEHRER
But now I can't fill out a poll.

   (A distant sound, again, of the same sort as before.)

JIM LEHRER II
(Starting, a little.) Did you hear that?

JIM LEHRER
Excuse me?

JIM LEHRER II
I heard something.

(They listen.)

JIM LEHRER
Maybe. I'm not sure.

JIM LEHRER II
It's gone.

JIM LEHRER
Okay.

(Beat.)

So your play tonight. It provoked a vigorous response.

JIM LEHRER II
Yes.

JIM LEHRER
Because of its being different to this that you wrote.

JIM LEHRER II
It was very different.

JIM LEHRER
How so? You see, I'm envious of the response your work received. My thought is to apply what you did to my efforts on this poll.

JIM LEHRER II
No. And I don't, like I said, I don't remember.

JIM LEHRER
But you ought to remember something.

(Again, a sound.)

JIM LEHRER II
(Starting.) What is that? There is someone there.

JIM LEHRER
How can you not remember your own play?

JIM LEHRER II
Someone is in the house.

JIM LEHRER
How can you not?

JIM LEHRER II
There was a sound.

JIM LEHRER
Did you manage any work on that poll at all?

JIM LEHRER II
THERE WAS A SOUND.

(Pause.)

JIM LEHRER
This old house makes sounds. It's oddly constructed.

JIM LEHRER II
Of course.

JIM LEHRER
Some of its rooms are entirely unsatisfied with their

current positionings. Ambitious to warp their way to another side—or level, even. The attic is always wanting to flap off into the hills like a moth.

JIM LEHRER II
This was not the sound of a moth.

JIM LEHRER
Well, what was it the sound of?

(*Pause.*)

What was it the sound of?

JIM LEHRER II
I don't know.

JIM LEHRER
You don't know. Just as you don't know your own writing. Just as I am helpless to know my answers to this poll. There is a great cloak of unknowing in this home. Help me. Help me. It will be shameful if that woman comes back and I've done nothing, nothing with what she left me. Help me.

JIM LEHRER II
What can I do? I can't fill out that poll. She handed it to you. She wants your answers, not mine.

JIM LEHRER
That's true. That's the truth. But look at this mountain of pages here that you birthed. They have to apply somehow.

JIM LEHRER II
I don't see how they would. It's an old draft of a play.

JIM LEHRER
But such a remarkable play. To drive the villagers mad.

JIM LEHRER II
That wasn't the result solely of any play.

JIM LEHRER
What? Oh, yes, your lights went catawampus and.

JIM LEHRER II
There is a fragrance of wickedness that has un-chambered itself on this evening. Do you not sense it?

JIM LEHRER
You seem an easily alarmed person, Jim. I'm surprised at this difference between us.

JIM LEHRER II
I'm not easily alarmed. I was attacked by a theater audience. All of them fully possessed, released from themselves. In their nerves and hearts capable of anything: murder, infanticide, sex with dead people, etc.

JIM LEHRER
And that is a remarkable thing. To have that sort of engagement. I hope to have equal success with this poll.

JIM LEHRER II
Success? This was not success. And in any case, a poll is not a play.

JIM LEHRER
I've got nothing else, Jim. And maybe I will surprise you. As you were surprised by the effect of your theater project.

JIM LEHRER II
But it's just a poll.

JIM LEHRER
Have you read it? It is as impenetrable as an alchemical incantation. Perhaps, as such, it has concealed powers.

JIM LEHRER II
All right. All right. I trust you. Your instinct. I'll help best I can.

JIM LEHRER
Thank you. Honestly.

JIM LEHRER II
What question has you stuck?

JIM LEHRER
Just about the whole run of them. But these first two about truthfulness and honesty are especially tricky. "On a scale of one / to ten

JIM LEHRER II
(Starting.) Do you not hear that?

(We've heard nothing here.)

JIM LEHRER
Hear what?

JIM LEHRER II
Off there.

JIM LEHRER
No, I don't. There is only the sighs of an old house and the grumblings of your sullen indifference to my new-born

aspirations.

JIM LEHRER II
A robe being placed to one side, perhaps. An animal's yawn.

JIM LEHRER
Those are different sounds.

JIM LEHRER II
Tree sap, stirring.

JIM LEHRER
Different.

JIM LEHRER II
And the same as before. The exact same.

JIM LEHRER
A clue to its unreality. Who would, or could, come into our home and not only make a sound that I can't hear, but, in addition, replicate that sound so precisely?

JIM LEHRER II
Shhh.

JIM LEHRER
Look. You've been moved to agitation by a nonexistent sound that I can't hear; this theater endeavor that you yourself have described as barely nothing, coaxed its audience to great feelings... why doubt the potential / of

JIM LEHRER II
Shhh!

JIM LEHRER

of my participation in this poll, a poll which in all likelihood has found its way to the sitting room tables of every house in this village? This is big stuff.

JIM LEHRER II

Now it's gone. Nothing.

JIM LEHRER

There was nothing.

JIM LEHRER II

We need to call for help. We need to find your phone or fix mine. Go with me to the pantry for rice.

JIM LEHRER

No. You are an imaginative person of the theater is why you are imagining things.

JIM LEHRER II

I'm going for a bowl of uncooked rice. I'm going to dry out my phone and call the police.

(He exits, with cleaver. Jim, alone:)

JIM LEHRER

Good evening. Jim Lehrer, alone, again. Some questions for future round table discussion and/or debate: One. What is the double of the Unknown? Two. What is the twin of Fear?

(Jim II re-enters. His cleaver is gone.)

JIM LEHRER II

My cleaver's gone.

JIM LEHRER
What was it about, generally?

JIM LEHRER II
I had it when I left and I didn't drop it. It was taken.

JIM LEHRER
Was it a happy, or what's the, a sad story?

JIM LEHRER II
My play?

JIM LEHRER
Yes, as it turned out this evening.

JIM LEHRER II
I've told you honestly I don't remember what.

JIM LEHRER
But it's so important to me, Mr. Lehrer, that you do. Remember.

JIM LEHRER II
How could it have just left my hand?

JIM LEHRER
There shouldn't be secrets between us.

JIM LEHRER II
I'm not keeping a secret. I don't remember.

JIM LEHRER
Then you're keeping a secret from yourself. Who are my friend and duplicate. So it's the same thing and exactly as bad.

JIM LEHRER II
They made it about a.

I don't know.

JIM LEHRER
What? What?

JIM LEHRER II
A man. A man who.

JIM LEHRER
What did he do? A man.

JIM LEHRER II
A man who wandered. And sang.

JIM LEHRER
A singing man.

JIM LEHRER II
A man who sang as he wandered. As he entered each scene.

JIM LEHRER
He sang? The song about being cold? From the page I found in the hall?

JIM LEHRER II
No, no. Some other song.

JIM LEHRER
But he sang.

JIM LEHRER II
In the distance, in the wings before he entered. But / look

JIM LEHRER

Like this?

(Exits.)

JIM LEHRER II

Jim? Jim, we've got to.

JIM LEHRER

(Singing while re-entering, not off-key, but to a just slightly different melody than the traditional.)

Happy birthday to you
Happy birthday to you
Happy / birthday

JIM LEHRER II

No, no

JIM LEHRER

to yooouuu
Happy Birthday to you.
Like that?

JIM LEHRER II

No, nothing like that.

JIM LEHRER

How can you not remember your own play?

JIM LEHRER II

That's as it should be. Who cares what a play is about? It should be as forgettable as a dream. A pale flickering. A stammer or shy wave of the wrist before the folding into cold oblivion.

JIM LEHRER
(Who exited after his last line and wasn't listening—he's further off now.) More like this? *(Again, slightly off, but in a different way.)*

Happy Birthday to you
Happy Birthday to you
Happy Birthday to yoooouuu
Happy Birthday to you

(He's re-entered. There's blood on his hand.)

JIM LEHRER II
Oh. You've cut yourself, Mr. Lehrer.

JIM LEHRER
What?

JIM LEHRER II
Your hand. There's blood.

JIM LEHRER
Oh. Oh, dear.

JIM LEHRER II
Let me wrap it.

JIM LEHRER
With your tie?

JIM LEHRER II
How did you do this?

JIM LEHRER
I don't know. Which is strange.

JIM LEHRER II
There is someone here. This is the evidence.

JIM LEHRER
I'm worried about your tie. The blood is going to wet right through it.

JIM LEHRER II
There is someone in this house.

JIM LEHRER
Oh, stop your worry.

JIM LEHRER II
Hold still. There.

JIM LEHRER
You're a good friend to me. I wish I remembered you more often.

JIM LEHRER II
What do you remember about your getting this cut?

JIM LEHRER
Nothing. It's like you with your play. Hey. Maybe it's something that happened in your play.

JIM LEHRER II
What, no.

JIM LEHRER
Wouldn't that be a twist. If we were by happy accident fashioning a replica of your play.

JIM LEHRER II
No.

JIM LEHRER
One that could be remembered.

JIM LEHRER II
No, I wouldn't want that.

JIM LEHRER
You don't want that? To remember your play? You don't *want* to remember your play?

JIM LEHRER II
I just. I think we have other concerns.

JIM LEHRER
Was this tie been in the creek? It's likely not sanitary.

JIM LEHRER II
I suppose.

JIM LEHRER
I should get a clean bandage or a poultice. From the cabinet.

JIM LEHRER II
No, no. There's no call to go out of this room.

JIM LEHRER
I won't be long. And I need a bandage.

JIM LEHRER II
There is someone there. Someone who just now cut you.

JIM LEHRER
Oh, no. I'm fine.

JIM LEHRER II
There's something off there.

JIM LEHRER
You work on remembering your play. On the wanting to remember.

JIM LEHRER II
Please, Jim, no. Don't go.

JIM LEHRER
You work.

JIM LEHRER II
No, no.

(Jim goes. Jim II gets a grip on himself.)

Jim Lehrer reporting, as of late, quietly. Some commentary:

Is there, in fact, a shadow—a double—of this world? And if not, what then is it we glimpse through the labyrinths and gossamer interlacings of matter that maturate on the stage? Surely the theater is not a lens, or a frame, or a mirror. Anything so useful as those would be more popular, and culturally consequential. No, the theater is a crevice. A crevice through which demons and all matter of ancient horrors may flow. From the shadow, the double, of this world.

(A distant sound. Jim II starts. Pauses. Listens. There's nothing more.)

What is in my mind?

This one thought rings:

There is no thing
that has no twin.

    (Jim enters, with bandaged hand.)

JIM LEHRER
That can't be true. Here's your tie back.

    (He holds it out. Jim II doesn't take it.)

JIM LEHRER II
Did you ever find how you hurt yourself?

JIM LEHRER
It was dark, I suppose. Splinters and ironwork poking all around.

Now I'm asking for your help with my poll. I'm going to sticky-up the paper with this hand.

JIM LEHRER II
Did you look for your phone?

JIM LEHRER
Have you a remembrance of your play?

JIM LEHRER II
Did you pass by the pantry for some rice?

    (Pause. Jim lets the tie drop to the floor.)

JIM LEHRER
I thought you had done that.

JIM LEHRER II
No.

JIM LEHRER
Yes, you went for rice and came back and reported your cleaver missing.

JIM LEHRER II
I had meant to, yes. I had meant to get the rice.

JIM LEHRER
Were you being untruthful? When you said.

JIM LEHRER II
No, no. I honestly intended to get the rice.

(*Pause.*)

JIM LEHRER
Are you me?

JIM LEHRER II
Pardon?

JIM LEHRER
If it had been me, promising rice, there would be rice. Here.

JIM LEHRER II
I'm Jim Lehrer.

(*Pause.*)

JIM LEHRER
Go on and get the rice, then.

JIM LEHRER II
No.

JIM LEHRER
And why?

JIM LEHRER II
Not safe.

JIM LEHRER
I just went. Just went and returned, freshly bandaged.

JIM LEHRER II
No, I'll stay. I can help you with your poll.

JIM LEHRER
You haven't been any help.

Go on for the rice.

How are we having this debate? If you're Jim Lehrer.

JIM LEHRER II
Folks debate themselves.

JIM LEHRER
That's true.

But if it were me, I would go for rice.

If it were actually myself.

And not a suspect version.

Go on for the rice.

JIM LEHRER II
If I go and get rice, then fix up my phone, can we go on and call the police?

JIM LEHRER
It's your phone. Got it two-for-one.

JIM LEHRER II
I will make some noise, cry out, if there's anything goes wrong.

JIM LEHRER
When you return here's what I'd like.

JIM LEHRER II
What's that?

JIM LEHRER
Come with a song. Enter singing. Try to remember and repeat that moment in your play.

JIM LEHRER II
I don't want to remember my play. How it was tonight.

JIM LEHRER
Make it the same moment. Cast back your mind.

JIM LEHRER II
No.

JIM LEHRER
You won't help me? Jim?

(Pause.)

JIM LEHRER II
I'll try. A song.

JIM LEHRER
I'll have my ear out.

(Jim II exits, with knife.)

JIM LEHRER
Some commentary:

Perhaps worthy of investigation is the question of how, in fact, I did cut my hand. Back in the darkness there. Do I take myself at my word that it was an accident of some sort? Or do I question the rigor, the honesty, of my account and suspect that indeed from here I went to the room of this house that holds my collection of knives, took a rare First World War Russian penknife *(He takes out a rare Russian penknife.)* from its wall mounting, pressed its blade against my left wrist and.

> *(Putting the blade to his wrist, making his strange, repressed cry.)*

AAhhrruuhh.

> *(Pause.)*

And then lost my nerve, faltered in my self-destruction. Became awkward as only the suicide lacking in resolve becomes awkward. The edge slipped to my palm and.

> *(Jim II re-enters. He's got the cleaver.)*

JIM LEHRER II
There is someone there. Brushed me in the shadows, took my knife, and pressed this cleaver into my hand.

JIM LEHRER
(Having hastily put the penknife down on the table.) Are you certain?

JIM LEHRER II
I'm holding this cleaver.

JIM LEHRER
But you weren't surprised? You didn't cry out or make a sound of any sort. Crept in quiet as the dew.

JIM LEHRER II
I am by nature an undemonstrative man. But I think I did. "Cry out."

JIM LEHRER
I didn't hear.

JIM LEHRER II
But you haven't heard anything all night long.

JIM LEHRER
I also didn't hear you sing. As we agreed you would.

JIM LEHRER II
There is someone off in there.

JIM LEHRER
You are not Jim Lehrer.

JIM LEHRER II
How can you / think

JIM LEHRER
If I wrote a play, I would remember what it was about.

JIM LEHRER II
You have only to look in my face.

JIM LEHRER

I've seen your face. I've heard your voice. Watched your gait, your limbs' movements. It's true there are remarkable commonalities with myself. But this night I've pushed the skin of my face right to the mirror of you. And up that near, the mirror goes blurry. You hear things I do not. You worry on things I've no concern over. And you have no vigor or can-do in regards to this poll, or its mysterious relationship to your forgotten play. You're no Jim Lehrer.

JIM LEHRER II

But you said you remembered me. It came back to you.

JIM LEHRER

Memory is but an acquaintance. And a doubtful one.

JIM LEHRER II

Oh, Jim. Jim.

JIM LEHRER

If I wrote a play I would remember it.

JIM LEHRER II

Again, the matter of my play is not of consequence. It is the events after, the audience's response / after the curtain

JIM LEHRER

I want you, I just would like for you to go out and return, singing. Go out and come on with a song.

JIM LEHRER II

No, no. I'm not going.

JIM LEHRER

(Pushing him out, not ungently.) Just go. Show me, Mr. Lehrer. Show me how it went.

JIM LEHRER II
(Threatening with the cleaver.) No, NO!

(Pause—a tense one.)

JIM LEHRER
I never understood how the evil twin could ever call himself a twin. In any honest way. It would seem to me his evil would set him apart. Make him alone. Singular.

JIM LEHRER II
(Lowers the cleaver.) I would just rather stay and help you with the poll.

JIM LEHRER
You are not Jim Lehrer.

JIM LEHRER II
I am. I am you. Please. *Please.*

JIM LEHRER
What's your business in my house?

JIM LEHRER II
I live here. As myself.

JIM LEHRER
Leave.

JIM LEHRER II
You remembered me.

JIM LEHRER
I don't know you, Mr. Lehrer.

JIM LEHRER II
Please. You're lonely. Please.

JIM LEHRER
Well, I've grown attached to my Loneliness. Please go.

JIM LEHRER II
I can help. With this poll. I can help.

JIM LEHRER
You've been no help. Go.

JIM LEHRER II
(Seeing the penknife.) What's this?

>   *(Pause. Holds it up.)*

Where did this knife come from? Why is there a new knife in this room?

JIM LEHRER
I took it from the collection. It brings me comfort.

JIM LEHRER II
Why were you holding it against your wrist when I came in as I have just now remembered you doing?

JIM LEHRER
I was thinking.

JIM LEHRER II
Thinking?

JIM LEHRER
I was thinking of your play and maybe something that happened in it. A knife against a wrist.

JIM LEHRER II
That wouldn't have happened / in my

JIM LEHRER
What did then happen in your play, / Mr. Lehrer? What did then.

JIM LEHRER II
I mean to say that wouldn't happen with *myself*. Jim Lehrer would never hold a knife against his wrist.

JIM LEHRER
I was thinking *of your play* / what it might have

JIM LEHRER II
Are you being honest with me? Are you being *factual?* No Jim Lehrer I know would do away with Jim Lehrer.

>   *(Pause. Jim breaks down, in effect confessing to the suicide attempt.)*

JIM LEHRER
I sat a-stage with presidents and their challengers. With the makers of this world. And now so alone. Looking back at that fleck of myself flickering in the distance of the past. So alone.

JIM LEHRER II
But I'm here. *I'm* here. *(Indicating the penknife.)* There's no call for this sort of business.

>   *(Pause.)*

Perhaps this evening has nudged us both a bit off-center.

JIM LEHRER
Yes. I'm not feeling myself. But I am still. Jim Lehrer.

JIM LEHRER II
As. Am. I.

(Pause.)

JIM LEHRER
I want that to be so.

JIM LEHRER II
It is.

JIM LEHRER
I want you to be myself.

JIM LEHRER II
As I would want the same.

JIM LEHRER
It's a terrible thing when things you think are you seem not to be.

JIM LEHRER II
Terrifying.

JIM LEHRER
A broken feeling.

JIM LEHRER II
Like with my play.

JIM LEHRER
Your play.

JIM LEHRER II
Just wasn't me. In no part.

JIM LEHRER
And I don't understand that. There must have been a bit of you floating in there. Something.

JIM LEHRER II
Not a bit.

JIM LEHRER
Only because you don't remember it.

JIM LEHRER II
I don't wish to remember. Like looking in a mirror and someone else is there.

JIM LEHRER
There must of been something in it of you. Of us.

JIM LEHRER II
Why don't we work on this poll.

JIM LEHRER
My poll? Oh, yes.

JIM LEHRER II
Let's just get it done.

JIM LEHRER
The poll. You know, I so appreciate that you've turned your attention to this poll of mine a number of times this evening despite the fact that, as you say, it really has nothing to do with you.

JIM LEHRER II
Well, yes. I mean, I know it's important to you.

JIM LEHRER
But you return to it, albeit reluctantly. It's on your mind as well.

JIM LEHRER II
It is. Because what's meaningful to you, because I am, in fact, you, also carries weight with me.

JIM LEHRER
Or maybe it's in your thoughts because. Because that's the connection to your play. What you remember.

JIM LEHRER II
No, I don't, well, what. What?

JIM LEHRER
Hold it in both your hands. Put down that cleaver. Hold it. Think now.

JIM LEHRER II
(Holding the poll.) What am I thinking?

JIM LEHRER
Is it possible, is it maybe the case that it was about the filling out of a poll? Your play. That would / explain

JIM LEHRER II
No no.

JIM LEHRER
That would explain your initial reluctance to help me / here, with this poll.

JIM LEHRER II
We really have to find your phone / or fix mine

JIM LEHRER
Don't you see. This poll is our shared circumstance. If it / was

JIM LEHRER II
There is someone / here

JIM LEHRER
if it was the subject of your story then there would've been a bit of me *a bit of you* in your play after all.

JIM LEHRER II
We have to investigate / the

JIM LEHRER
Humor me. Humor me. Allow that it might've been what your play was about.

JIM LEHRER II
A play about filling out a poll on a village council election?

JIM LEHRER
Is that a rule of the drama? That a scenario can't concern a questionnaire?

JIM LEHRER II
Well, no, I suppose it may / but

JIM LEHRER
With this poll I hope to *reestablish communication with life.* It seems to me that your play or theater house had that same hope.

JIM LEHRER II
No, I don't know. No.

JIM LEHRER
Every activity should have that same hope. The *reestablishment of communication with life.*

JIM LEHRER II
I want to preserve my life. From whatever, whoever it is that's just outside this room.

JIM LEHRER
Maybe, maybe it is your enigmatic main character, the singing man. Looking for his moment to enter.

JIM LEHRER II
No, no, the characters, the actors were all left back at the theater. It's the audience / that

JIM LEHRER
He's singing because he's joyful. He's joyful because he's entering the room where a political poll—hard copy— waits on a table for him to mark. He has a task, a purpose, and from the purpose springs the song, and the song drives the purpose. *The song drives the purpose.* I'll perform at being the man again.

(*Jim exits.*)

JIM LEHRER II
No, no, stay.

Please stay with me here. Far from the theater. Don't. Don't make it one with your entrances and.

(*Attempts to gather himself.*)

Report.

Jim Lehrer.

> *(Picks up the poll.)*

Was this my play? What it became tonight?

"On a scale of one to."

No. It's what it should have been. Straightforward and inoffensively inquisitive. A reflection of myself. Another me on the stage. But no. It was.

It became.

JIM LEHRER
(From off, the scream of one getting his throat cut.) AAAHHH!

> *(Silence.)*

JIM LEHRER II
Mr. Lehrer?

> *(A distant sound is heard.)*

Jim?

Jim?

JIM LEHRER
(Singing—to the proper melody—the bridge to "We Three (My Echo, My Shadow, and Me)" from offstage as he enters:)

What good is the moonlight
the silvery moonlight

that shines above
I walk with my shadow
I talk with my echo
but where is the one I love?

> *(He has entered. Strangely, his hand is free of its bandage and there's no sign of the wound.)*

Like that. It happened like that.

JIM LEHRER II
What happened?

JIM LEHRER
I'm telling you.

JIM LEHRER II
Excuse me?

JIM LEHRER
The song and the entrance. It / happened

JIM LEHRER II
No, what happened just now, out there. Back in there.

JIM LEHRER
I'm just trying to report the relevant facts. The song, what it was, how it / was sung

JIM LEHRER II
There was a cry. You cried out.

JIM LEHRER
Mr. Lehrer, Jim, all due respect, you're not the reporter. You don't have the eye or ear for what's germane to a story.

JIM LEHRER II
Where is your bandage?

JIM LEHRER
The which?

JIM LEHRER II
On your hand. You had a cut on your hand and a bandage.

JIM LEHRER
Oh, that. Earlier I found a kit of yours back there with little props and theatrical makeup—rubber noses and goatees and so forth—and thought I'd try out some of your stage blood. That's all that was. I just now washed it clean.

JIM LEHRER II
But I'm a playwright. I don't have a makeup kit or / rubber nose or

JIM LEHRER
Well I certainly don't have an actual cut on my hand.

JIM LEHRER II
I wrapped that cut myself. With my tie.

JIM LEHRER
Yes, I remember. You, playing along. Here's the tie. Does that look like actual blood to you? Would you, a man of the theater, who knows little of war zones and world crises even know real blood to look at it?

JIM LEHRER II
There is no makeup kit or stage blood in this house.

JIM LEHRER
That's true, isn't it. I made that up. I was not honest.

(Pause.)

Why don't we complete this poll.

(Takes up the poll and pencil stub and easily answers each question.)

Alright. Okay. Yes. A six. Eight. No. Don't know. Three. Three. And no.

Good.

That is how it happened, you know.

JIM LEHRER II
How which happened?

JIM LEHRER
The entrance.
I walk with my shadow
I talk with my echo...
The song and the entrance. I'm giving a factual report. But that's all that's stuck with me. Your work is not memorable, Mr. Lehrer.

JIM LEHRER II
You were not there. At my play.

JIM LEHRER
Anyone can be at a play. That's the special power of the modern audience: they are cloaked in darkness. Among their bodies there may be anybody. They are the mystery. The shadow.

JIM LEHRER II
You were not there.

JIM LEHRER
I wonder if there's a body back there. In the hall or foyer. A body in its own darkness, bleeding out. Whose face is not discernible in its darkness, but which you might trace with your fingers and conclude its shape and lines to be not dissimilar to your own. Our own.
It's possible. I don't remember.

JIM LEHRER II
His body's back there?

JIM LEHRER
Who now?

JIM LEHRER II
My. My friend.

JIM LEHRER
It wasn't easy, let me tell you. Finding this place. Neither of you wanted anything to do with me. The Double of the Double. Shadow of the Shadow. But then you put on a play. And anyone can come to a play. And rile up the audience.

A cough and grumble from the back.

JIM LEHRER II
You.

JIM LEHRER
That sparked the commotion? Hard to know. Might well have been your lighting mishap. When things get wild, when the Gates of the Permissible swing wide, not sure who to chide, the show or the show-goers.

(A distant sound. Jim Lehrer is mildly puzzled at this.)

JIM LEHRER
Huh.

JIM LEHRER II
You followed me home.

JIM LEHRER
Where someone left the porch light on. For his lady pollster's return. Hoping to engage with the world. And here I come. Part of the world, anyway.

(He calmly tears up the poll.)

I think both political parties are really just exactly the same, don't you?

JIM LEHRER II
His body's back there?

JIM LEHRER
I'm not sure. My memory, gasping and button-eyed as a decked fish. Maybe it's just been you and me the whole long day.

(For the last time, a distant sound.)

Why don't you investigate? Come back with a report.

JIM LEHRER II
No.

JIM LEHRER
Are you going to flee? Make a run for it? Either deeper into the house or out into the world's shadow-strewn waste.

I should tell you, that world is somewhat shifted from

when you, or he, rather, sat a-stage and asked questions of presidents and their challengers. New monsters have come. From under the mirror.

Oh, some sort of nut.

(He takes an almond.)

Going to later make me thirsty.

Run, Mr. Lehrer. Run.

(Jim Lehrer II runs away.)

(Jim Lehrer sits.)

(The lights slowly fade until all we can see is his face.)

(The doorbell rings.)

(The lights fade to black as Brenda Lee's version of "We Three (My Echo, My Shadow, and Me)" plays.)

END

MICKLE MAHER is a co-founder of Theater Oobleck and has worked in Chicago as an actor, director, and playwright since 1987.